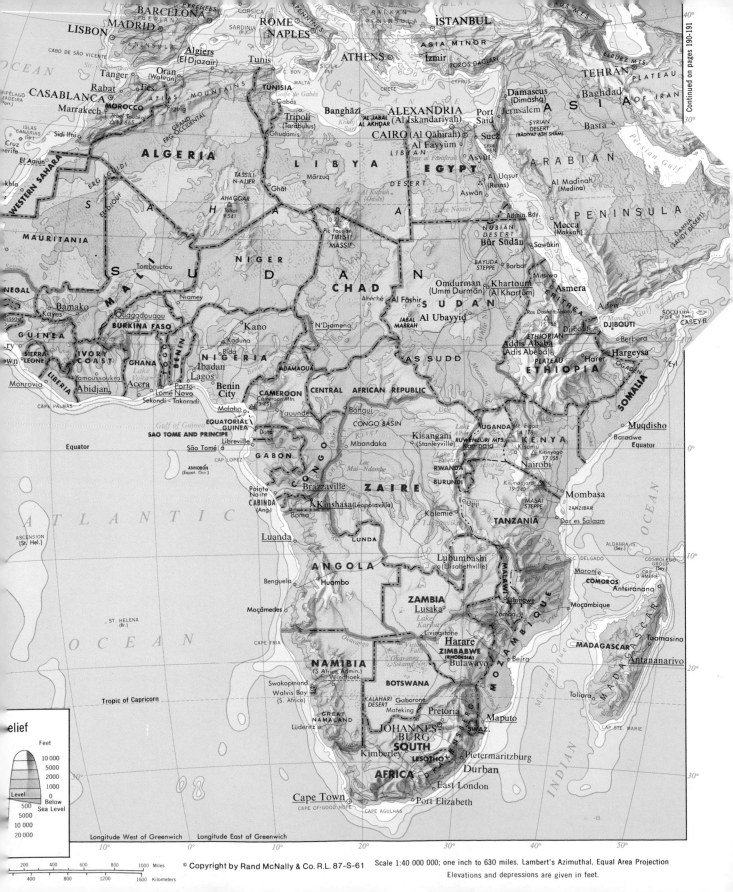

5° 10° 15° 20° 25°

El Djazaïr
Algiers • **El Boûlaida**
Tizi-Ouzou
Khemis • **Bejaïa** **Skikda** **Annaba**
Qacentina □ (Bône)
Stif Guelma
Batna Béja
S TELLIEN Chott el Hodna Menzel
Bourguiba
A T L A S **Tbessa** **Bizerte**
M O U N T A I N S **Beskra** Jebel Chambi **TUNISIA**
ATLAS SAHARIEN 1544 Kasserine
• Laghouat Chott **Kairouan** • **Sousse**
Melghir ▼40 Gatsa Moknine
• **Ghardaïa** El Wad 23 Tozeur **Sfax**
Touggourt Chott Jerid ÎLES KERKENNA
Médenine Golfe de Gabès
Gabès
ÎLE DE JERBA
Zuwārah
El Menia
Hassi Messaoud Remada Az-Zāwiyah **Ţarābulus**
Wargla Tripoli
Nālūt Al-'Azīzīyah Al-Khums
Gharyān Tarhūnah Zlītan
Yafran **Mişrātah**
• Mizdah Bani Walīd

ALGERIA GRAND ERG ORIENTAL
Ghadāmis Dirj T A R Ā B U L U S
H A M Ā D A T T R I P O L I T A N I A
PLATEAU DU TINGHERT Al-Qaryah
TINGHERT ash-Sharqīyah
Ohanet Sawknah
Bordj Omar Idriss JABAL AS-SAWDĀ
In Amnas • Zillah
Tiguentourine
Edjeleh Sabhā Birāk A L - H A R Ū J A L - A S W A D
• Ilizi Awbārī **Fazzan** **Fezzan** L I B Y A
TASSILI-N-AJJER S A H Tarbū
• Salah Al-'Uwaynāt • Marzūq
• Ārak Ghāt Wāw al-Kabīr
A H A G G A R Djebel Teleriheba Djanet SAHRĀ MARZŪQ R A B Y Ā N A H
Tahat 2420 Al-Qatrūn
2908
• Tamenghest

ÎtaIy
Palermo Messina
Marsala • **Reggio di Calabria**
ISOLE EGADI Trapani Monte Etna 3323
Caltanissetta SICILIA I T A L Y
Agrigento SICILY
I. DI PANTELLERIA Gela **Catania**
Ragusa **Siracusa**
CAPO PASSERO
GHAWDEX Ionian Sea
MALTA **Valletta**
ISOLE PELAGIE
(It.)

KEFALLINÍA **Pátrai** **Athínai**
Korinthos Athens
Zákinthos Pírgos **Piraiévs**
PELOPONNISOS Spáti
Kalamai **GREECE**
ÁKRA TAÍNARON ÁKRA MALÉA
KÍTHIRA Kritikón Pélagos
Khaniá **Iráklion**
Ídhi Óros
2456
CÁVDHOS KRITI CRETE

KIKLADHES NAXOS
AMORGÓS
MILOS

KHÍOS
SÁMOS Aydin
ÁNDROS TÍNOS IKARÍA Den
DHODHEKANISOS
Bodrum
RÓD
KÁRPATHOS

M E D I T E R R A N E A N S

Al-Baydā' Darnah
• **Banghāzī** Al-Marj
Suluq Tubruq
Bardiyah Sidi Barrani
Musaid As-Sallūm
Marsá Matrūh
Khalīj Surt Abyār al-Ḥakīm
Surt
Marsá al- • Ajdābiyā B A R Q A H
Burayqah C Y R E N A I C A
Al-'Uqaylah Al-Jaghbūb
• Dahra 47 ▼ MUNKHAFAD AL-QAṬṬĀR
Marādah ▼133
Awjilah Siwah
AṢ-S
AL-GH
Waha WESTERN
Bī'r al-Harash DESERT
ṢĀḤRĀ Al-W
Qaşr al-Farāfira
al-Far
H A R A
Bī'r al-Harash
• Al-Jawf
o Ma'tan Bishrah
AS SAHRĀ AL-LĪBĪYAN DESERT
Jabal al-'Uwaynāt
1934

Tropic of Cancer
TASSILI TA-N-AHAGGAR Oued Tamanrasset
In Guezzam
Grêboun 1944
Chirfa Pic Tousside Bardaï Bette 2266
3315 Aozou T I B E S T I
Zouar
A Ï R Séguédine Emi Koussi
Herouane 3415 Ounianga Kébir
Bagzane DÉPRESSION DU MOURDI
2022
N I G E R Bilma Faya E N N E D I
Ingal GRAND ERG DE BILMA • Fada
• Agadez T É N É R É BODÉLÉ
Tahoua Oum-Chalouba
Illéla Tânout
Birni Nkonni C H A D
Ingal Nguigmi • Mao S U D A N
Maradi Tessaoua **Zinder** • Gouré Bahr el Ghazal Abéché Al-Junaynah **Al-Fāshir**
• Sokoto Lake Chad Moussoro Maiha W
Lac Tchad
(281)

Enchantment of the World

LIBYA

By Marlene Targ Brill

Consultant: Lisa Anderson, Ph.D., Middle East Institute, Columbia University, New York City

Consultant for Reading: Robert L. Hillerich, Ph.D., Bowling Green State University, Bowling Green, Ohio

CHILDRENS PRESS ®

CHICAGO

In the desert (above) are great stretches of plateaus and sand dunes, but some areas, such as Tripoli (opposite page), are rich in vegetation.

Library of Congress Cataloging-in-Publication Data

Brill, Marlene Targ.
   Libya.

   (Enchantment of the world)
   Includes index.
   Summary: Discusses the geography, history, religion, economy, people, and everyday life of the North African country.
   1. Libya—Juvenile literature. [1. Libya]
I. Title. II. Series.
DT215.B75 1988   961'.2   87-13192
ISBN 0-516-02776-X

FOURTH PRINTING, 1994.
Childrens Press®, Chicago
Copyright ©1987 by Regensteiner Publishing Enterprises, Inc.
All rights reserved. Published simultaneously in Canada.
Printed in the United States of America.
   4 5 6 7 8 9 10 R 96 95 94

Picture Acknowledgments
Shostal, New York City: Pages 4, 12 (right), 17 (top), 25, 26, 79 (left), 84 (right, top and bottom), 85 (left), 92, 95, 99 (top), 104; © D. Forbert: Cover, Pages 6, 56, 74 (bottom), 79 (right), 91 (top)
Hutchison Library: Pages 60 (top), 85 (right); © B. Regent, Pages 5, 12 (left), 19 (left), 24, 28 (left), 86 (bottom), 90 (left), 91 (bottom left), 93 (top left), 96, 97, 107
AP/Wide World Photos: Pages 8 (2 photos), 48 (left), 51, 53 (2 photos), 55 (2 photos), 59, 114
Woodfin Camp & Associates: © Robert Azzi: Pages 9 (right), 11, 86 (top), 90 (right), 93 (bottom left), 100 (top right); © Pierre Boulat: Pages 10 (2 photos), 17 (middle, left and right), 18, 37 (2 photos), 74 (top), 78, 81, 82 (2 photos), 84 (left), 93 (right, top and bottom), 94 (2 photos), 100 (bottom left), 109, 113, 115
Photo Researchers, Inc.: © Robert Isear: Pages 9 (left), 76, 99 (bottom); © Kazuyoshi Nomachi: Pages 14, 68, 100 (bottom right); © George Holton: Page 32 (left); © Tom Hollyman: Page 34; © O. Martel: Pages 63 (left), 66, 89 (left), 98 (left), 100 (top left), 105
© **Cameramann International, Ltd.:** Page 19 (right)
Animals Animals: © Margot Conte: Page 21 (left); © J.A.L. Looke: Page 21 (right)
UPI Photo: Pages 23, 32 (right), 40, 42, 43 (2 photos), 44, 45, 46 (2 photos), 48 (right), 89 (right)
Historical Pictures Service, Chicago: Pages 28 (right), 38 (2 photos), 60 (bottom), 62, 63 (right), 67 (2 photos), 72
Photri: Page 69
H. Armstrong Roberts: Page 91 (bottom right)
The Photo Source: © Three Lions: Page 98 (right)
Len W. Mcents: Maps on pages 14, 95
Courtesy Flag Research Center, Winchester, Massachusetts 01890: Flag on back cover
Cover: Burning off natural gas

TABLE OF CONTENTS

The Old City of Tripoli

Chapter 1

A NEW COUNTRY
WITH OLD TRADITIONS

CELEBRATION OF OLD AND NEW

September 1 is a special day for Libyans. The national holiday marks Libya's Revolution Day, the anniversary of the day in 1969 when Muammar al-Qaddafi and his small group of military men calmly ousted King Idris. Equally important, the day signifies the beginning of change for Libyans. Discovery of oil had transformed Libya's poor economy into one of great wealth. Independence from Italy in 1951 had given Libya the right to self-government, but the 1969 revolution altered every other segment of Libyan life.

Throughout history, there have been many battles on Libyan soil. Phoenicians, Greeks, Romans, Turks, and Italians all fought to rule the land and its people. Some of the most critical battles of World War II were waged in Libya's vast desert. And when the sands settled, Libya was to become an independent nation for the first time—a nation ripe for change.

The revolutionary government celebrates Revolution Day with grand military parades in all the cities. Tripoli, the nation's capital, holds the longest parade, lasting four to five hours. The parade slowly winds along the scenic coastal road on the

Part of the celebration of Revolution Day

Mediterranean Sea. Air and naval troops pass down city streets as crowds cheer. Groups of schoolchildren follow in athletic formations amid marching bands.

Banners and flags wave from buildings. Libyans take pride in their green rectangular flag. Green is the color of the Islamic religion. Qaddafi even chose that color for the *Green Books* he wrote, which are the basis for today's Libyan government.

Libyan men, children, and a sprinkling of the more modern women pour into the streets dressed in their best to see the parade. Revolution Day is similar to the Fourth of July in the United States. There are firecrackers and a rousing closing speech by Qaddafi. Like other holidays in Libya, it is a family day with wonderful celebrations.

HOLIDAY DRESS

Most Libyans who live in cities wear European clothes. However on special occasions, such as holidays, they are proud to wear the native dress that rural Libyans and older women always wear.

Traditional Libyan women are never seen in public. They wear veils over their faces, and *barracans* to cover their bodies. They

*Some men (left) wear fezes and barracans, togalike
blankets, as part of their national dress, while most women
cover their faces (right) when they are in public.*

fasten at the left shoulder and under the chin and wrap the body
in a blanket of white from head to toe. Only one eye views the
world. Underneath, women wear a costume of a brightly colored
shirt and loose pants drawn in at the ankles. Shoes are actually
slippers that come to a point in the front, and are open in the
back.

Libyan women like to wear jewelry. Gold necklaces presented
by grooms to their brides are worn for feasts and entertaining.
Other necklaces and bracelets have the "protective hand of
Fatima," Prophet Muhammad's daughter; a silver fish or amber
beads. These symbols are protection against evil.

Men wear barracans, too, which date back to the Roman togas.
They are made of wool for winter, and cotton for summer. But
men do not need to cover their faces, unless they are from remote
Touareg tribes. Barracans protect the loose pants and shirt the
men wear underneath. The excess serves as a hood in bad
weather. Some men wear a *fez*, a small felt hat, as part of their
national dress.

Oranges (left) and fresh bread (right) for sale at a market in Tripoli.

TRADITIONAL FOODS

Libyan mothers stay home from the festivities to prepare the midday meal. The main meal of the day is usually at 2:00 P.M., before the afternoon rest. Shops and schools close from two to five every afternoon when there is no holiday. On Revolution Day, the temperature could rise to 120 degrees Fahrenheit (48.9 degrees Celsius) by midafternoon. The heat will tire those watching the parade. After eating only rolls and tea for breakfast, the family will be hungry for a large meal.

On Revolution Day, the holiday meal will probably include the national dish, *cous-cous.* Women make cous-cous by kneading wheat flour, water, and salt into tiny balls. Then they cook the cous-cous and a separate combination of vegetables and lamb. The final dish looks like a volcano on a large platter. The vegetable mixture lies in the center of piles of cous-cous. Plain cous-cous sweetened with milk and honey is eaten for breakfast.

Sheep provide lamb, the most common meat on Libyans' tables.

Libyans eat lamb more than other meat. Pork is forbidden by Islamic law. Meat is ritually slaughtered by a Muslim butcher after he recites a prayer from the Quran, the Muslim holy book. Lamb is usually eaten at the midday meal. Dinner, served later in the day, is a lighter meal of cheese and yogurt.

Mothers prepare the national drink, tea, for the holiday meal. First, they boil it in a kettle until it is very dark. Roasted hazelnuts and plenty of sugar are placed in the bottom of special small cups. Then the brewed tea is poured from high above the cup so a layer of foam forms. Children and adults enjoy the sweet drink with meals and after siesta.

ENTERTAINMENT

Children enjoy the day off from school on Revolution Day. After their meal and rest, they go about their work and play. Those who live in suburbs might collect dates from palm trees or oranges from someone's orchard. Some children watch television.

Girls have more household chores than boys. They cook or sew. But they also like to play a version of hopscotch or other games in the garden.

Local musicians dressed in traditional costumes

Boys have more freedom. They go to the market daily for fresh
vegetables and fruits. On the way, they play soccer in the streets,
schoolyard, or garden.

Older boys gather in groups. They drive around the city or go to
movies. Before the revolution, there were movie houses offering
films from everywhere. Now films are mainly from India and
Egypt. In fact, there are generally fewer forms of recreation since
the revolution. The government discourages Western
entertainment, which it says contributes to laziness. It also frowns
upon spectator sports, but soccer is still popular at the university.

For special occasions, men and women have traditional dances.
These are simple dances of hopping from side to side. Drums,
tambourines, and bamboo flutes play national songs in the
background. Dances and music remind Libyans of their tribal
roots. Primitive music tells of shifting desert sands, nomadic life,
and historic coastal cities.

Chapter 2

THE DIVIDED LAND

Ancient nomad tribes first gave Libya its name in prehistoric times. As the tribes scattered, Libya's boundaries expanded.

By the time Greeks settled the area during the seventh century B.C., all of North Africa except Egypt was called Libya. To the east, the old Libyan border was less than five miles (eight kilometers) from the Nile River in Egypt. Western boundaries extended to the Atlantic Ocean.

Today, Libya's eastern border lies almost 400 miles (644 kilometers) west of Cairo, Egypt. The country occupies 679,362 square miles (1,759,540 square kilometers) in the center of the North African coast of the Mediterranean Sea. Libya's Mediterranean coastline runs 1,047 miles (1,685 kilometers). To the west are Algeria and Tunisia. On the south are Niger and Chad. Sudan shares a small part of Libya's southeast border.

For the size of the country, Libya has few people. The nation is the fourth largest country in Africa and the fifteenth largest in the world. It is two-and-a-half times the area of Texas. Yet, the population is about 4.5 million.

Most of the country is desert. Extreme heat and dryness make most of the land unlivable. Ninety percent of the people live on less than 10 percent of the land, mainly along the Mediterranean coast.

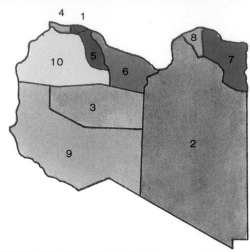

PROVINCES OF LIBYA
1. Tarābulus
2. Banghāzī
3. Sabhah
4. Az-Zāwiyah
5. Al Khums
6. Misrātah
7. Darnah
8. Al-Baydā
9. Awbārī
10. Gharyān

Libyans and their camel stop for a rest in the desert

LAND MOLDS HISTORY

Geography has played an important role in Libya's development. The Mediterranean coast linked European countries across the sea with North African Arab countries. Lively urban cities sprang up throughout history as many European visitors came to join caravans, trade goods, or buy and sell slaves.

In contrast, the vast desert, the Sahara, isolated rural tribes. Few people traveled the sandy wasteland. Farming was possible on sparse oases only. Tribal chieftains ruled without interference from foreign influences. As a result, many tribal customs linger among desert people to this day.

There are several hilly regions in Libya. The highest elevation is in the Sarīr Tibasti in the south and southwest desert near Chad. Here, Bette Peak rises 7,500 feet (2,286 meters) above sea level. Lower slopes of 3,000 feet (914 meters) appear south of Tripoli and east of Banghāzī along the coast. Just south of the coast is a narrow semidry grassy plain that is ideal for farming. Between these productive regions is the Gulf of Sidra.

The barren desert stretches north for 311 miles (500 kilometers) from the Sarīr Tibasti to the sea.

Some historians say that this emptiness, called the Surt Desert in the north, and the Gulf of Sidra have altered the course of history for Libya. These two barriers of land and water contained the spread of ancient Phoenician and Greek colonies along the Mediterranean coast. They provided natural separations that divided Libya into three regions: Tripolitania, Cyrenaica, and Fezzan. Each region differed according to the land and life-styles that developed there. Strong differences persisted until 1969. At that time, the revloutionary government renamed these regions.

Tripolitania became Western Libya; Cyrenaica became Eastern Libya; and Fezzan became Southern Libya. These new regions were divided into the provinces of Tarābulus, Banghāzī, Sabhah, Az-Zāwiyah, Al Khums, Misrātah, Darnah, Al-Baydā, Awbārī, and Gharyān. But the old names continue to be references today.

TRIPOLITANIA

Tripolitania, the area west of the Surt Desert, has grown in much the same way as the North African countries of Tunisia, Algeria, and Morocco. These areas bordering on the Mediterranean Sea are so similar in history that they are often referred to collectively as the Maghrib.

Tripolitania covers about 16 percent of Libya's land area and has the nation's capital and largest city, Tripoli. For centuries, Tripoli was the central terminal for caravans crossing the desert trade routes, and gave shelter to pirates and slave traders.

Tripolitania's Mediterranean coast extends 186 miles (300 kilometers) from the Surt Desert westward to Tunisia. Along the coast, grassy areas interchange with sandy plains and lagoons. This land is one of the most important agricultural areas of the country.

The entire coastline is broken by *wadis,* river valleys that are dry except during the rainy season. Along some wadis are remnants of Roman construction. The Romans built dams and aqueducts to control what water was available for their homes and farms. In addition, wadis protected the Roman colonies by hindering east-west travel.

Today, the government has built new dams in wadis to reserve rainwater and for flood control. Many people live and farm along

Above: Even in the mountains and plateaus, such as the plateau of Jabal Nafusah, rainfall is rare. Below: Modern machinery (left) and irrigation (right) are used in the cultivation and harvesting of wheat.

wadis because the soil is more fertile. In the early 1970s, one survey found fifty-one major wadis in Libya.

Somewhat inland is the Al Jifarah plain, a triangle-shaped area of about 5,792 square miles (15,000 square kilometers). Farther inland about 75 miles (120 kilometers) is a steep cliff rising to form the Jabal Nafusah, a plateau that rises to 3,280 feet (1,000 meters). Wide fertile valleys within the plateau allow the growth of grains on the slopes.

A modern office building in Banghāzī

CYRENAICA

The area just east of the Surt Desert was named Cyrenaica.
Wandering tribes originally settled the area. In the nineteenth
century, these tribes were united by the the Sanusi Muslim
religious order, much like other Arab countries of the Middle East.

Cyrenaica includes the entire eastern part of Libya. It runs from
the Mediterranean to the border of Chad, covering 51 percent of
Libya's land area.

The Cyrenaica coast curves away from the Surt Desert into the
Mediterranean. The 130-mile (210-kilometer) arch connects the
two cities of Banghāzī and Darnah. Except for the Bay of Tubruq,
this coastline is smooth.

South of the coastal area rises the Al Jabal al Akhdar (Green
Mountain), which is really not green at all. Instead, this is a rocky

Left: Professionals are employed to climb date
trees to pick the fruit. Right: Nomads in the desert

plateau almost 2,900 feet (884 meters) high. The plateau extends
the width of the coastline from Banghāzī to Darnah and slopes
gently south into the part of the Sahara called the Libyan Desert.
All of Libya's heavy rain falls on the plateau. Leafy pine, juniper,
and cypress trees have been growing here for centuries. That's
how the plateau earned its name. In addition, vineyards and fruit
trees wrap the northern slopes. On the southern slopes are
woodlands that shrink into shrubs and grass. Then the grasses
disappear into the desert.

FEZZAN

Most of southwestern Libya, Fezzan, is desert. Because of the
barrenness of the desert, the people of Fezzan have traditionally
been nomads. Nomads are people who wander from place to place
in search of food and water for themselves and grazing land for
their flocks.

Nomadic leadership has usually been tied to tribes. To this day, ties are close with black African tribes in Chad, Niger, and Mali.

Fezzan occupies 33 percent of the country. Only the Sarīr Tibasti mountains break the dull land. Except for date trees and cactus thriving on oases, there are great patches of plateaus and sand dunes without vegetation.

PLANTS AND ANIMALS

Throughout Libya, many cacti, date, and palm trees grow wild. The cactus is Libya's national plant. Children like to pick the prickly pear cactus fruit and eat the sweet, pulpy inside, seeds and all.

The national animal is the *waddan*, which is a male gazelle. It's not unusual for someone living in the country to look out the window and find a waddan in the backyard. The animal is so popular that a major hotel in Tripoli has the same name. Outside the hotel's main entrance is a fountain with a sculpted gazelle.

There are many different kinds of wildlife. There is a variety of birds from small doves and finches to larger eagles and vultures. In the coastal marshes are ducks, plover, terns, and gulls. In the waters are turtles, lobsters, and crawfish to catch for food.

Nevertheless, the desert harbors some of the most unusual animals. Many species of mice and rats survive the sweltering heat by *aestivation*, a kind of hibernation. They sleep all summer, the way a bear sleeps in the winter. By aestivating, animals, nighthawks, and some insects conserve energy and their need for food.

One small desert rat called the *jerboa* attracted attention during

A waddan (left) and a jerboa (above)

World War II. It reminded the Australians in the British Eighth
Army of home. The jerboa, with long hind legs, leap like tiny
kangaroos. The Australians liked them so much they made the rat
their emblem and nicknamed their division the Desert Rats.

WEATHER

Libya's climate varies with nearness to the sea and desert and
land elevation. Coastal regions have a climate similar to other
Mediterranean countries. Sea breezes bring mild temperatures.
Summers are warm and winters mild.

Temperature can climb to 115 degrees Fahrenheit (46 degrees
Celsius) in the summer. Often, the weather is humid and
unpleasant. Southern breezes blow hot winds from the desert. The
highest temperature ever recorded anywhere was 136 degrees
Fahrenheit (58 degrees Celsius) in Al Azīzīyah, Libya, on
September 13, 1922.

Winters are much cooler. Temperatures average 46 degrees Fahrenheit (8 degrees Celsius). In the mountains, weather is more extreme. Sometimes, frost can be seen on the mountaintops.

There is little to the spring and fall seasons. Summer seems to plunge into winter. However, these short times of year bring the dreaded *ghibli*. The ghibli is a strong, hot, dusty wind that blows from the south for one to four days. The wind whisks the desert dust across the countryside, leaving a red-brown smothering cloud. High winds raise the rough sand 3 to 6 feet (.9 to 1.8 meters) above ground. With the dust come quick temperature rises, which usually destroy crops. Desert winds can raise temperatures in only a few hours. Days are oven hot, with only a little cooling at night.

Rain gives little relief. Most of the rainfall is in the winter, but the season is short. When rain comes, mainly along the Tripolitania coast, it brings whipping winds and driving torrents. Northeastern Libya may receive up to 20 inches (51 centimeters) of rainfall a year. The rest of the country has much less rain.

Lack of rainfall is a continual problem for Libyans. Without rain, there are no permanent rivers or lakes. Small streams form during the rainy season, but vanish during the many long, hot months. Droughts ruin crops every few years.

To monitor the water supply, the government has a special Secretariat of Dams and Water Resources. Water is so important that the government fines or imprisons anyone found damaging a water supply.

Most Libyan water comes from shallow underground wells. The wells tap water between layers of rock. Even with these wells, only about 6 percent of the land is suitable for farming. Ninety percent of the land is desert.

A cave drawing, thought to date back to 5000 B.C., shows a man driving a chariot with wheels.

THE DESERT

Sahara means desert in Arabic. Some geographers label all North Africa from the Atlantic to the Red Sea as the Sahara. However, the northeastern portion located in Libya is called the Libyan Desert.

The Libyan Desert was once a grassy prairie. Rock drawings from prehistoric people show elephants, giraffes, and 9-foot (2.7-meter) birds that look like ostriches. The wildlife has since moved to central Africa. The rich grasses have turned to burning sands, leaving oases and tribal communities dotting the golden sand.

Oases are palm-covered areas where shade and underground water can be found. Nomadic Bedouins come to oases at certain times of the year as they move with their herds in search of pasture. Not too many years ago, oases provided rest from the

An oasis

harsh desert for camel caravans through the desert. Now they
may be sources for oil, or rich farming communities producing
dates, figs, olives, grain, and citrus fruits.

Explorers have always been curious about the desert. They have
felt its fury, also. Throughout the centuries there have been stories
about caravans of people marching into the desert never to be
heard of again. Were they burned by the sun or covered by a
sandstorm? Did they lose their way or run out of food and water?
These were all dangers of the desert.

The desert is still treacherous. In the desert, it is difficult to
judge distance, size, and shapes. There are no physical objects, like
trees, to use as reference points. There are mountainous
formations. Some look like pictures of the surface of the moon.
But there are no shadows. There are no sounds, except the
occasional whirling of shifting sands against rocks and the singing
of tribespeople to break their loneliness.

The shifting sands of the desert

The only signs of previous life are old bones from birds that could not last the trip migrating north. Birds have been following the same desert route since prehistoric times, when the area was rich with vegetation. Their habit is instinctive.

Travelers, hot from the sun, may see a *mirage*, or vision, of an endless lake of blue water. Scientists say this illusion is a reflection from the sky. Some travelers have even seen illusions of trees or buildings in the distance.

The desert can be a dangerous place, but it also can be beautiful. Dawn comes up in mauve, purple, and gold before daylight disperses the color. During the day, the desert is bland and drab. But at sunset, the orange sky makes the sand glisten.

Arabs are proud of the desert. They say that in the cool evenings God walks and thinks in silence undisturbed. Arabs also like to quote an old Arabic saying. "He who has seen the desert three times always yearns to go back."

Ruins of a Greco-Roman theater in Cyrenaica

Chapter 3

A CONQUERED NATION

Many people have been drawn to Libyan borders because of its central location on the Mediterranean. As a result, the country has been under suppression continually.

Until independence, Libya was always ruled by foreign powers to some degree. Between 1050 and 1382, there were fourteen conquests of the area.

Conquerors divided the land and the people. The people from Tripolitania, Cyrenaica, and Fezzan had different roots. They followed different leaders. There was no one single political unit called the Libyan government.

Yet little remains from the ancient cultures of the Phoenicians and Romans. There are marvelous ruins at the ancient cities of Cyrene, Leptis Magna, and Sabratah. But traditions have passed through the generations.

The Libya of today reflects its chaotic past. Culture is built upon culture to instill customs and ideas.

EARLIEST LIBYA

Archaeologists trace the first Libyans back to 8000 B.C. Along the coastal plain, Libya shared the same primitive culture

*A Berber fortress (left) and a drawing of
a Berber woman (right) from about 1885*

common to other Mediterranean regions. People farmed and
raised cattle. They invented and used stone tools.

To the south, wandering herdsmen tended their flocks in the
well watered grasslands that were to become the Sahara. Ten-
thousand-year-old drawings on cave walls show hunters chasing
rhinoceroses and elephants, animals that have been gone for
centuries. Culture thrived until the creeping desert and powerful
invaders scattered the people southward or into Berber lands.

THE BERBERS

Berber origins are unclear. Some historians say they were
originally from southwest Asia and moved into Africa in about
3000 B.C. Others say they were from North Africa.

Berbers were an unusual people. They never had one nation.
They spread over North Africa and later became part of the Arab
world. But they kept their devotion to family, tribe, and
community. They preferred to be called *imazigham*, or free men.

Only spoken language bound Berbers together. They had no alphabet or written language. Tales of their history were passed from one generation to another by storytellers. Hence, the true story of their past became lost.

An Egyptian inscription from about 2500 B.C. tells of a Berber tribe called Lebu, or Libyans, that raided as far east as the Nile. The tribespeople settled there and served the Egyptian pharaohs.

By 950 B.C., Shishonk I, a Berber, took control. He began a succession of Berber pharaohs from 950 B.C. to 720 B.C. These rulers were known as the Libyan dynasty.

Since Berbers had no written language, their history was told by the ancient writers of Greece and Rome. They called all Berber lands Libya. Some of their accounts tell of Berber customs that are similar to those practiced today.

PHOENICIANS IN TRIPOLITANIA

By about the seventh century B.C., Phoenicians had become the chief traders on the Mediterranean. They built safe harbors for their ships from the countries bordering the northeast Mediterranean to Spain. Many cities in North Africa, including some Libyan towns, began as Phoenician trading posts.

To move into Libya, Phoenicians had to make peace with Berber tribes. These treaties helped the Phoenicians gain rich Libyan raw materials of ivory, ebony, and ostrich feathers.

During the next two centuries, three Phoenician settlements were established in Libya: Oea (Tripoli), Labdah (Leptis Magna), and Sabratah. Together these three cities became known as Tripoli, or Three Cities.

GREEKS IN CYRENAICA

As Phoenicians secured new trade, Greeks sought to expand their colonies. Legend says that an oracle from the shrine of Delphi ordered people from the crowded island of Thera to find a new home in North Africa.

Berber guides led the islanders to what is now Cyrenaica. They told the Greeks that just inland there was a "hole" in the heavens. There they would find plenty of rainfall and fertile land for farming.

In 631 B.C., Greeks founded the city of Cyrene, the capital of Cyrenaica. The city prospered as a Greek trade and cultural center. Cyrene grew to 100,000 people.

Life was good in Cyrene. Aristippus, the philosopher, founded the Cyrenaic school of philosophy and education. People learned the meaning of happiness and reason. Cyrene also had a medical school, several academies, and fine architecture. Archaeologists have found remnants of Cyrene's lifestyle in ancient marble baths, temples, and burial grounds under desert sands.

Other Greeks joined those from Thera. In the next two hundred years, they settled four more main cities that became present-day Al Marj, Banghāzī, Tūkrah, and Apollonia. With Cyrene, the cities were known as Pentapolis, or Five Cities. The entire area later took the name Cyrenaica after the principal city of Cyrene.

Farther Greek expansion into Phoenician land was blocked by the Surt Desert. However, there is an interesting story about the border. Legend says it was actually set after a deal was made between rulers of the two countries.

The border was to be the point where runners from Phoenicia's Carthage and Greece's Cyrene met. However, myth suggests that the Greeks did not believe the Phoenician runners, the Philaeni brothers, could run so fast so far. The brothers offered to be buried alive to prove Phoenicia's honor. From that day, the Altars of Philaeni over their grave marked the Tripolitania-Cyrenaica borders.

GARAMENTES IN FEZZAN

Foreign settlers stayed near the coastal plains while the Garamentes ruled the Fezzan deserts. The Garamentes were a powerful tribe who conquered the area in about 1000 B.C.

Not much is known about the warlike Garamentes. Some historians believe they were Berbers. Their wealth and technical skill can be seen in the ruins of their stone towns and pyramid tombs.

The Garamentes controlled much of the desert caravan trade. Phoenicians used them to carry gold, ivory, and slaves from the western Sudan to the Mediterranean. Greeks and Romans sometimes battled with the Garamentes. Other times there were treaties with their war chiefs.

ROMANS CONQUER LIBYA

Fighting left Tripolitania and Cyrenaica open to Roman invasion. The population of Rome was expanding, and the military growing. Rome needed Libyan soil to grow wheat for food. By the first century A.D., after a military and trade pact with the Garamentes, Romans occupied the coastal regions of Libya.

Tripolitania and Cyrenaica prospered during the five hundred years under Roman rule. For the first time, their citizens shared a common language and laws.

Left: The floor of this sixth-century Byzantine church was discovered in 1957.
Right: This type of well has been used since 100 B.C..

Large and small cities had the comforts of urban life. There were markets, entertainment, and baths, which were common in other parts of the Roman Empire. Merchants from around the world came to North Africa. And the Romans built roads and armies to protect their interests. Archaeologists have uncovered ruins of Roman city life along the Mediterranean coast.

Yet the most important legacy from the Romans was Christianity. By the end of A.D. 400, Roman colonies in Africa were all Christian. The large Jewish population staged revolts. Other people of Libya rebelled against the Roman bishops. Seeds of Libyan religious and social revolt were planted.

VANDAL AND BYZANTINE RULE

More than five hundred years of Roman rule ended in the fifth century A.D. German barbarians called Vandals sacked the European and North African Roman empires.

Vandals were cruel to Romanized Berbers in urban areas. They were so ruthless that the word *vandal* became the term for recklessness and destruction.

Gradually, Vandals made North Africa their home. They intermarried with Phoenicians, Berbers, and Romans. After many years, their presence was feared less.

Meanwhile, the new Roman Empire of Byzantium grew stronger. In 535, Byzantines overtook all Vandal towns. At that point, Vandal history ended.

Byzantine rule restored much of the order lost under the Vandals. Upper- and middle-class people spoke only Latin at home. Roman clergy returned with their Christianity. So did Berber resistance to this religion.

Byzantine governors collected high taxes to support a military for protection against Berber attacks. Without money for city services, such as a water system, cities like Cyrene and Tripoli became neglected.

About the same time, camels replaced donkeys for desert travel. Camels were quicker and could carry more goods. Camels also made it easier for nomadic Berbers to raid Byzantine farmland. Byzantine armies often left their fortified cities to march against the invaders. But the tribespeople would flee on camel into the desert or mountains. This unusual warfare lasted until the late seventh century. However, true freedom was far away.

Arabs, traveling by camel, spread the word of Allah.

Chapter 4

INTRODUCTION

OF ISLAM

After two centuries of Byzantine-Berber fighting, religious followers of the Prophet Muhammad took over the Byzantine colonies. Their rule marked one of the most important eras in Libyan history. This was a time when all signs of Christian and European culture disappeared.

Muhammad preached a reform religion of Islam. He believed in a single, all-powerful God, Allah. Muhammad called upon believers to make the individual, family, and government second to the laws of this God. The word Islam means *submission*. Followers of Islam are called Muslims, "those who submit to God's will."

According to Islam, those who die fighting for their religion are blessed. Thousands of Arabs left the Arabian Peninsula by camel to bring the word of Allah to the Western world.

The time was ripe for conquest. The Persian Empire to the east and the Roman Empire in the west were decaying. Their colonies were too vast to govern. Local people in the colonies still resented foreign rule.

Arab conquest met with little resistance. Warlike Berbers slowed the Arab advances, however. But by 710, Arabs had seized Cyrenaica, Tripolitania, and Germa, the capital of the Garamentes, and pushed west to Morocco and north to Spain.

Unlike previous rulers, Arabs saw themselves as missionaries rather than colonists. They stayed in the lands they conquered, and married local people to entrench their culture. With Arabs came the Arabic language, Islamic religion and government, and a new way of life.

Most people converted to the Muslim faith. Pagans were given the choice of "Islam or the sword." Converts received land and tax benefits. Christians and Jews who did not convert were taxed, but otherwise were left alone. Muhammad recognized these groups as the first religions. For all their religious fervor, the Arabs were tolerant rulers.

During the next few centuries, Libya experienced a Golden Age along with the rest of the Arab world. Arabs repaired the neglected irrigation systems and brought new life back into the cities. Libya prospered again. Life was relatively calm—at least for a while.

From the eleventh to the thirteen centuries, various Western countries sent armies to reclaim the Holy Land, Christ's birthplace, from the Muslims. The Crusades, as they were called, were unsuccessful. But they did weaken Arab power.

After the battles, many Crusaders settled in Mediterranean coastal cities. King Ferdinand of Spain captured Tripoli in 1500. The Catholic king urged his Crusaders, known as the Knights of St. John, to remain in the city. They stayed until they were chased out by the Turks in 1551.

The Archaeological Museum in Tripoli, with a serpent fountain in its courtyard, was originally the Red Castle, built as the seat of government of the Ottoman Turks. It later became the headquarters for the Italian government.

BARBARY PIRATES

The Ottoman Turks called the North African countries of the Maghrib the Barbary Coast. The Turks adapted the name from the Berber tribes who still populated North Africa.

Libya was a Barbary state, along with Morocco, Algeria, and Tunisia. All these countries were home to Barbary pirates. And pirate captains were usually local governors, or *pashas*.

Piracy had always been a problem for ships sailing the Mediterranean. But by the sixteenth century, the Turks expanded piracy into big business. One story puts the number of captives held for ransom in Tripoli, Algiers, and Tunis at twenty-five thousand.

Many of the most famous pirates were Christian outlaws. They

Barbarossa (left) and a ship (above) used by the Barbary pirates

paid casual tribute to Allah and the sultan of Turkey for the privilege of raiding under Turkish protection and living like government officials. The military may have ruled, but their loyalty went to whomever paid and fed them the most.

One famous Greek traitor was Khair al Din, or Barbarossa. He captured Algiers in 1510, pretending to defend it from the Spaniards. In turn, he acknowledged the Ottoman sultan and was made governor. Barbarossa expanded Ottoman power in the Maghrib and sacked many coastal towns before he died in 1547. Yet his way of working set the pattern for future pirate captains.

Captains, or *raises*, had such large businesses they formed corporations, or *taifas*. These corporations gave captains a stronger voice in government to help carry out their trade. Powerful captains took over ports and established rule. They called themselves *deys*, or representatives of the Sultan in Constantinople.

Captains lived well. They dressed in grand clothes and lived in large, fortresslike villas. Inside, the rooms displayed a mixture of European and Oriental bounty. Lower floors housed slaves and servants to maintain the kitchen. The master lived with his harem and closest allies on the upper floors.

Pirates supplied the Turkish government with a steady income. Their sleek, swift ships constantly overtook larger merchant ships. Pirate crews would board these foreign ships, steal their cargo, and enslave the crew.

Wealthy captives were usually released for ransom. Poorer captives had to give up their Christianity for Islam to go free. Most wound up either as slaves at auction or on ship crews. From the pirate's booty, 12 percent went to the port overlord, 1 percent was a harbor fee, and 1 percent went to the local mosque.

Pirates constantly fought each other, but they united to battle Christians in the Western world. One Turkish pirate, Ahmed Karamanli, brought some calm to the jealous fighting. He conquered Tripoli in 1710. His family ruled Tripoli and parts of Cyrenaica for one hundred years.

During the Karamanli's rule, Tripoli grew to a city of fourteen thousand people, with gardens and beautiful white buildings. It became a major trade port from Sudan and central Africa. Spices, ostrich feathers, hides, gold, and slaves were shipped across the Mediterranean. Finally, family feuding and European plotting with local pirate captains ended the Karamanli order.

THE BARBARY WARS

By the eighteenth century, Barbary pirates were uncontrollable. Thieves wanted any foreign country sailing the Mediterranean to pay a tax, or tribute, for safe passage. Otherwise, they captured the ship and enslaved the crew.

The United States fought back in what became known as the

In 1803, the United States Marines shelled the Red Castle in Tripoli. The interior is new; the outer walls still stand.

Barbary Wars from about 1801 to 1805, and again in 1812. The fighting was more like raids than full-scale war. At first, attacks by sea failed. Then William Eaton, the American consul to Tunisia, organized a small battalion of United States Marines and four hundred Arabs who wanted the dey out of Tripoli. They would cross the desert and attack by land. They marched for over a month before reaching Cyrenaica and capturing Darnah.

Eaton's action forced the pasha to make peace with the United States and free American prisoners. Nevertheless, pirates continued to bother passing ships until the end of the War of 1812. U.S. Navy ships bombed the last pirate fortresses into ending their attacks.

ITALIAN COLONIZATION

Ottoman Turks controlled Libya until Italians chased them out in 1911. But the Italian government found parts of Libya particularly difficult to repress.

One group of resistors was led by Omar Mukhtar, a leader of an Islamic sect of the Sanusi religious order popular among Cyrenaican Bedouins. Mukhtar was a Bedouin scholar of the Quran who taught in oases. He led a national underground resistance movement that enraged the Italians. Eventually, he was caught and executed. His story is told to all Libyan schoolchildren in history books.

Italians were opposed by many nationalist leaders of the Sanusi order. The Sanusi order was founded by Muhammad bin Ali al Sanusi. He was a great Islamic scholar and teacher. Tribespeople of Tripolitania and Fezzan called him Grand Sanusi (al Sanusi Al Kabir).

The Grand Sanusi believed in the purity of early Islam. He preached from his home in Cyrenaica about a unified Islamic community.

Cyrenaican tribespeople liked his traditional Islamic message. Their way of life had changed little since they first became Muslims centuries ago. When he died in 1859, the Grand Sanusi had made most of Cyrenaica's feuding tribes loyal to one religious leader.

Italian takeover met with Sanusi resistance from Cyrenaica, southern Tripolitania, and the Fezzan, as well as opposition from other groups. However, the Sanusis had the strongest organization. By 1916, the Italians thought it wise to negotiate with Sanusi leadership, which included young Muhammad Idris al Sanusi.

Italy managed the three Libyan territories as separate colonies. They gave Idris almost complete control over inner Cyrenaica. Tripolitania wanted the same freedom but lacked Sanusi organization. Italians made Fezzan a military territory.

The Sanusis, and other religious notables, were fiercely opposed to rule by Italians. Mussolini, on horseback, receives the Sword of Islam and promises religious freedom to the Muslims.

By 1922, a movement for independence was underway in Tripolitania. Nationalists offered Idris leadership of Tripolitania. His acceptance signaled open war with the Italians. They were threatened by his newly expanded power. Idris then fled to Egypt for safety. There he continued to direct the Sanusis.

ITALIAN RULE

In the same year that Tripolitania openly sought independence, Benito Mussolini became prime minister of Italy. Mussolini had his own plans for the three regions. He wanted the area made into a colony that would provide resources for the homeland.

Italian troops marched into Sanusi territory within the year. Cyrenaica was the site of the fiercest battles. Northern Tripolitania fell within a few years. Italy waged war for nine years

Left: In 1937, Mussolini was already preparing for war. Right: After the outbreak of war in 1939, Libyan horsemen and others worked together to get rid of the Italian forces in their country.

before all regions were defeated. Anyone opposing occupation was put into concentration camps. Many people died from Italian cruelty.

Mussolini officially called his colony Libya, its ancient name, in 1934. He divided Tripolitania and Cyrenaica into four provinces of Tripoli, Misrātah, Banghāzī, and Darnah. Fezzan remained a military post into World War II. Then he abolished all tribal councils in favor of Italian government. Only Italians held high positions.

Mussolini's goal was to build a model Fascist colony. He needed Libya to relieve Italian overpopulation and unemployment, so he sent thousands of settlers to live there. As an attraction, he poured large amounts of money into highways, trains, irrigation, and ports to modernize cities. By 1940, 110,000 Italian immigrants made up 12 percent of the Libyan population.

An Italian family who settled in Libya to farm

Italians brought medical care and improved sanitation to updated urban areas. But they gave little else to Libyans. There was no education for Arabs to become skilled workers. Life for Libyans in the city stayed much the same.

Rural Libyans fared worse. The most fertile tribal grazing lands were given to settlers. And Sanusi leadership was scattered outside the country, at least for the present.

WORLD WAR II

The outbreak of war in Europe in September 1939 gave Libyan nationalists the chance to repel Italy. Tripolitanian and Cyrenaican leaders met to work together. Differences between the

In 1942, the British hoisted the Union Jack at Tubruk after they had defeated the Nazis.

two groups ran deep. Nevertheless, they decided Idris should be leader of their cause.

Nationalists believed that their best hope for ridding themselves of Italians was to work with Great Britain and its allies. Maybe Britain would press for independence after the war.

To gain British support, Tripolitania and Cyrenaica offered volunteers for their military. The Libyan Arab Force, or Sanusi Army, fought bravely under British command.

The war was long and costly for Libya. The conflict destroyed most improvements made by the Italians. Some of the more important battles of World War II were fought in Tubruk, Darnah, and Banghāzī. Many times the course of the war shifted in the sands of Cyrenaica. Still, Libyans fought until the last Italian forces left Libyan soil in February 1943.

Above: Before education was available for everyone, "wise men" would write letters and fill out forms for a fee.
Left: The United Nations flag flew above the Grand Hotel in Tripoli until 1952.

Chapter 5

THE MAKING OF
MODERN LIBYA

INDEPENDENCE AT LAST

Postwar Africa desperately wanted freedom from colonial rule. Libya was no different.

As Italian troops fled, Britain occupied Tripolitania and Cyrenaica. French forces moved into Fezzan. Idris returned from Egypt. However, he would not settle permanently until foreign control was limited. Libya's fate at the end of the war was in the hands of the United Nations.

Italy gave up all claims to Libya in a 1947 peace treaty with the Allies. Britain quickly urged its friend, Idris, to take control of the government in Cyrenaica. On November 21, 1949, the United Nations decided that all of Libya would become independent before 1952.

Britain and the other Allies eased Libya into self-government. Most Libyans could not even read or write. They were uneducated

King Idris (left) rarely used this palace (right) in Tripoli because of his preference for his homes in Cyrenaica.

about politics. Libya was a poor nation with no sign of change. Equally important, Libyans were used to being ruled by foreign powers. Leadership had to be developed and a constitution written.

THE NEW GOVERNMENT

Libya became the first country to gain independence through the United Nations on December 24, 1951. King Idris became chief of state over the constitutional monarchy, to be followed by his heirs.

The new federal government consisted of a prime minister and two houses of legislature. The king appointed the Chamber of Deputies, or lower house. The Senate, or upper house, included eight representatives from each of the three provinces. Half of these people were named by the king, also.

Idris had considerable power as king. He could veto laws, dissolve the Chamber of Deputies, appoint local governors, and adopt emergency measures at will.

Local authority was left largely to the individual provinces. However, tribal loyalties persisted, and the three regions continued to vie with each other and with the federal government for power. To be neutral and to encourage national unity, the seat of government alternated from Banghāzī in the summer to Tripoli in the winter.

Government under Idris was generally conservative and stable, despite infighting. When there was strong political opposition, he abolished political parties.

Idris had good relations with other Arab countries and with the West. Libya became a member of the League of Arab States, and later founding member of the Organization of African Unity, promoting economic well-being.

The United States and Great Britain were primary supporters of agricultural and educational development programs to help improve Libya's poor economy. In return, Idris allowed the two powers to have military bases in Libya. In 1956, Libya was admitted to the United Nations.

Idris's government received an added boost when oil was discovered in 1959. Outside investors developed the oil industry and gave 50 percent of the profits to Libya in taxes. For the first time in its history, Libya had a future as an independently wealthy nation.

In the decade following independence, Idris realized Libyans needed to develop loyalty to their central, rather than provincial, government. Otherwise, Libya would not survive as a nation. He abolished the three historical divisions of Tripolitania, Cyrenaica, and Fezzan. Instead, he divided the provinces into administrative districts, each managed by an appointed governor. The town of Al-Bayda in Cyrenaica became the new seat of government.

OVERTHROW OF THE GOVERNMENT

Idris's new government found opposition on many fronts. First, Tripolitanians still mistrusted him. After all, Idris had historical ties to Cyrenaica. His followers were loyal to him as leader of the Sanusi order, rather than as Libyan king.

Second, Libyans found little relief from oil revenue. Wealth remained in the hands of a few at the expense of workers.

Third, many Libyans called for more involvement in the larger Arab world. They opposed Idris's pro-Western leanings. And they listened to radio broadcasts by Egyptian President Nasser. Nasser called for Arab nationalism and the creation of a Palestinian homeland.

Idris felt removed from much of Libya's population after eighteen years of rule. He began spending more time at his palace in Al-Bayda.

On September 1, 1969, when Idris was out of the country for medical treatment, about seventy young army officers took over the government without bloodshed. Other army units supported the action. No resistance was given to ending the Libyan monarchy. The day is celebrated as Revolution Day.

The group credited with the coup was called the Free Officers Movement. It was run by the twelve-member Revolutionary Command Council (RCC), which formed the base of government after the takeover.

The RCC proclaimed the country a free state named the Libyan

Muammar al-Qaddafi

Arab Republic. Their motto was "Freedom, Socialism, and Unity." With this slogan, they pledged to remove backwardness and promote equality for all Libyans. They adopted an Arab form of socialism that joined Islamic doctrine with social, economic, and political reform.

On the foreign front, the RCC remained neutral to the superpowers. They opposed Western imperialism and Russia's antireligious communism alike. The RCC called for Arab unity. They promised to take a role in aiding Palestinians and other Arab countries against Israel.

Within a week, the RCC selected an eight-member Council of Ministers to carry out its plans. Then they announced that twenty-seven-year-old Captain Muammar al-Qaddafi would become colonel and commander-in-chief of the Libyan Armed Forces. In reality, he was official head of state.

QADDAFI AND LIBYA

Muammar al-Qaddafi was the perfect choice for RCC leadership. He had energy, a dynamic personality, and an appealing appearance. Above all, he was a devout Muslim who followed a puritanical moral code. Qaddafi's ideas and policies became the driving force of Libyan politics.

Historians trace Qaddafi's philosophies and world views to his youth. His family lived in tents in the desert of Fezzan. They were part of a small Arabicized nomadic tribe of Berber origin who farmed and herded. They worked hard to find enough money for Qaddafi to go to strict Muslim schools.

He learned to be proud of his Arab and Libyan heritage at these schools. Later, he would be one of the few Arabs to wear native dress abroad when he went to Great Britain's Army Signal School near London.

Egyptian teachers and Nasser's radio show, ''Voice of the Arabs,'' fueled Qaddafi's nationalism as a teenager. When he was fourteen years old, he was expelled from school in Tripoli for organizing a student strike in support of Nasser's fight with Great Britain over the Suez Canal. Tutoring helped him finish school. He was graduated from the Libyan military academy and spent six months in England on a signals training course. But the fires of rebellion sparked early.

Qaddafi and the RCC patterned their revolution after Nasser's coup in Egypt. Arab unity became his chief quest, as with Nasser. Nasser's enthusiasm was eventually tempered by political reality. Qaddafi still pursues his dream.

Within weeks after the takeover, Qaddafi sent representatives to Egypt and Sudan to propose unity for the three states. Soon after,

Qaddafi (left) at a news conference in a tent at the army barracks in Tripoli in 1981 and in 1986 (right). Qaddafi generally wears traditional dress or his military uniform.

he proposed a merger of Egypt and Syria in the Federation of Arab Republics, and another with Tunisia. All offers failed to gain support.

At home, Qaddafi's nationalism was more successful. Thousands of Jews and Italians were tried and expelled. Relations with the West worsened. Even with promises of neutrality, the United States and Great Britain left their bases. Final pullout from the United States' Whellus Air Force Base signaled a Libyan national holiday in June 1970.

The new government built a welfare state within a few years. For the first time, it distributed oil money to take care of people's basic needs. Individual income in the first decade of Qaddafi's power brought Libya to one of the highest standards of living in the world.

The government also took over foreign-owned banks and agencies and expelled oil company executives. What little free press existed under Idris came to an end. Radio, television, and the three newspapers became ways to advance revolutionary causes. Radio was especially appealing, since so many Libyans who could not read or write had one. The ban on political parties remained. Arabs were restricted from any non-Islamic influences.

Qaddafi officially dissolved the Sanusi religious order in favor of his own traditional Sunni Muslim faith. He replaced the old judicial system separating religious and secular law with religious courts. *Sharia*, sacred Islamic law, became the guiding force behind the Libyan court system.

THE CULTURAL REVOLUTION

By 1973, Qaddafi had become dissatisfied with Libya's lack of revolutionary spirit. He introduced a five-point program called the Cultural Revolution. Essentially, his program marked a return to pure Islamic thinking, rejecting all other views. It had a new constitution reinforcing more "direct democracy."

The unique part of his program was the establishment of people's committees to allow Libyans more power in the decision-making process. People's committees became responsible for local and regional administration. They allowed people to rule themselves directly, without parties, parliaments, or other forms of representation.

The General People's Congress (GPC), as of 1977, provided central government for the Socialist People's Libyan Arab Jamahiriya, Libya's new name. The word *jamahiriya* means "state of the masses." The GPC has 1,112 delegates who meet twice a year to set national policy. Power still remains with Qaddafi. He and the other RCC members haven't held a formal meeting since the formation of the new government.

The political revolution was detailed by Qaddafi in *The Green Book, Part I: The Solution of the Problem of Democracy.* With *The Green*

The younger Libyan women are being liberated. Some even attend the military academy and are learning how to use submachine guns (left). Right: Students, in uniform, march in a military parade.

Book, Part II: The Solution of the Economic Problem—Socialism, he attacked any form of employee-employer relationship as slavery. He believed that no one should work for anyone else. His solution to this inequality was to eliminate wages in favor of partnerships. Everyone has a direct share in what is produced and its income.

Qaddafi believed every man had the right to one house, one vehicle, and an income. More possessions were unnecessary and should be turned over to people's committees. Ownership of more than one house or rental property was forbidden. Businesses were taken over by the state. Savings accounts above 1,000 Libyan dinar (then about $3,400) had to be given to the government. People were afraid to show they had any wealth.

Many urban middle-class and technical experts left the country as a result of these laws. Clergy who opposed the new program lost their religious land (*waqf*) and mosques.

Further opposition came after a ruling that everyone between the ages of seventeen and thirty-five should spend three years in the military. Qaddafi believes he must protect the gains his country has made.

Building a pipeline in the desert

The Green Book, Part III: The Social Basis of the Third Universal
Theory explores Qaddafi's thinking about history, society, women,
religion, and family. He views nationalism as a combination of
feelings for family, tribe, and ethnic groups. He defines each of
these areas in a general and historical way. Clear-cut direction is
yet to come.

Even with growing general opposition to his views, Qaddafi
still enjoys considerable support among Libyans.

FOREIGN POLICY

Libyan oil helped Qaddafi carry out his foreign policies. Oil
became the wedge he and other oil-producing Arab nations used
to equalize relations between developing and industrial nations.
He urged higher prices. He cut oil supplies. And he gained more

attention than normally accorded a leader of a few million people—because of Libyan oil wealth.

Oil profits support Arab causes. Libya's central foreign policy continues to center on the creation of an Arab Muslim nation-state. Two factors affect where this money goes.

First, Libya believes Arab unity can only be achieved by eliminating Arab leaders who oppose it. Some say Libya has tried to kill leaders, or has supported revolutionary groups in Morocco, Tunisia, Jordan, Sudan, and Egypt. Libya even moved its army into Chad, changing the tide in its civil war. Both Chadian sides joined forces to rid themselves of Libyan invaders.

Second, Libyans tie Arab nationalism to the return of Israeli land to Palestinians. Libyans are strong supporters of Palestinians finding their own homeland in Israel. Hostility against Israel continued into the 1990s.

Oil revenues helped strengthen Libya's military, which uses weapons bought from the Soviet Union. In the late 1980s the combined personnel of the army, navy, and airforce totaled nearly 85,000. Older people, women, and teenagers form a people's militia.

Qaddafi supports liberation movements around the world. However, his role in terrorism is unclear. Libya has been called a depot for Soviet weapons needed for African and Middle Eastern revolutions. Some say that Qaddafi has a part in underground activities as far away as Northern Ireland, South Africa, Italy, and Thailand. Yet post-Soviet Russia has taken a strong stand against violence and condemned Libya's terrorist activities in the 1990s.

In the 1980s, the Reagan administration in the United States claimed a strong link between Libya and terrorism. As early as 1982 an embargo was placed on oil imports and the sale of technical equipment. American travel to Libya is banned.

In December 1985, President Reagan imposed further economic and political sanctions against Libya for its supposed role in terrorist attacks on the Rome and Vienna airports, which killed twenty people. Within a month, he declared Libya a threat to the United States' national security and foreign policy. He severed all economic and political ties with Libya, and ordered the remaining 1,000 to 1,500 Americans in Libya to leave.

Tensions mounted. The United States' Sixth Fleet held maneuvers in the Gulf of Sidra. Libya considered this an invasion of its territory. The West accepts a 12-mile- (19-kilometer-) wide coastal strip of the gulf as belonging to Libya. Libya considers the entire 150,000 square miles (388,498 square kilometers) of the gulf to be within its boundaries. The United States and Libyan forces clashed in the questioned waters. After Reagan stated that Qaddafi meant to attack United States diplomats worldwide, the United States bombed Libyan missile sites.

Reagan hoped that confrontation would prompt the Libyan military to remove Qaddafi as their leader. However, the attacks seemed to strengthen Qaddafi's declining position in Libya and the North African and Arab world.

The following April, a bomb ripped through a West Berlin discotheque visited by American troops. Two people died and 155 were wounded, including about 55 Americans. United States officials strongly believed Libya was involved.

Shortly after, the United States mounted an air attack on Qaddafi's compound, naval academy, and air bases in Tripoli and Banghāzī. Stray bombs hit a residential neighborhood, the French embassy, and barracks where Qaddafi's family lived. The assault left fifteen people dead, including Qaddafi's young daughter, and sixty people wounded, including two of his sons.

Damage caused to homes and autos by United States planes in April 1986

Terrorism has caused many friends to back away from Libya. Some previous allies have closed their embassies in Libya and expelled Libyan diplomats.

LIBYA'S FUTURE

Reactions to Qaddafi are mixed. Westerners think he is a crazy religious extremist. Many Africans find him a strong leader. Libyans at home are generally satisfied as long as he continues to use oil money to improve their standard of living. An oil glut in the 1980s brought a slowing of government services. Increased outbreaks of unrest followed.

Yet, oil may be sapping the very national fires Qaddafi is trying to fan. People have become accustomed to free education and health care, increased wages, and housing aid. They are less willing to risk these improvements for revolution. Clearly, Libya's future will depend upon Qaddafi's strength and an ongoing oil supply.

Above: A mosque in Tripoli
Left: A European depiction of
Muhammad, holding the Quran

Chapter 6

LAND OF ALLAH

Religion plays a large role in the way Libyans live. Their daily routines, laws, government, and their view of the world are all reflections of the teachings of Allah, their God. No aspect of modern Libyan society is untouched by the traditional Muslim past.

BEGINNING OF ISLAM IN LIBYA

Islam first began in ancient times in Arabia. Nomad tribes believed in idols and nature. One of these tribes, the Quraysh, moved into the city of Mecca, bringing their religion.

Mecca was on a major caravan route from present-day Syria and Egypt to Yemen. There, the Quraysh established a booming trade center. They also built the Kaaba, the best-known Arabic shrine. The shrine drew rich and poor alike to the city.

In about A.D. 570, a Quraysh merchant named Muhammad began to question the worship of idols. He hated the inequality of life in Mecca in the name of religion. When he was forty, he began to have visions when he was alone in the desert. These visions came to him from God. He claimed they called him the prophet of God.

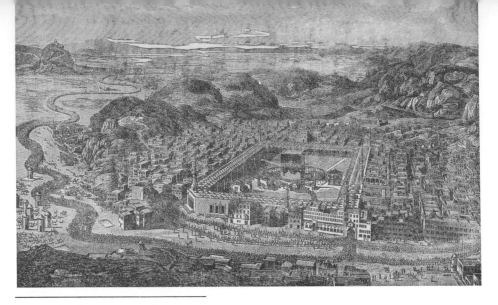

Mecca in the seventeenth century

Muhammad preached more and more against idol worship. He urged his followers to pray to one all-powerful God, Allah. Further, he called upon them to believe in him as God's messenger. Muhammad traveled widely along the caravan routes spreading Islam. And as he traveled, he learned from Jews and Christians, the original "Children of the Book."

Muhammad's teachings angered the people of Mecca. He and his followers had to flee Mecca for Yathrib, where his teachings were accepted. The city became known to Muslims as Medina, or "the city." Muslims mark his flight, or *hijra*, in 622 as the beginning of Islam history. The Islamic calendar begins with that year.

Muhammad fought the people of Mecca by attacking their caravans and continuing to preach. By 630, his followers returned to Mecca. They destroyed the idols and turned the pagan temple into a Muslim house of worship. The people then accepted Islam, with Muhammad as their spiritual leader. Mecca and Medina became Islamic sacred cities.

After Muhammad's death in 632, *caliphs*, or Muslim rulers, spread the word of Islam. They launched holy wars that brought conquests throughout the Middle East and North Africa.

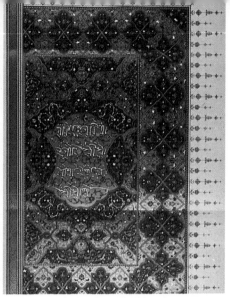

The holy book of the Muslims is the Quran.
Above: A portion of a sixteenth-century Quran
Left: Muslims discussing the Quran

Arabs easily swept over the Byzantines on Libyan land. They quickly replaced the customs in Libyan urban centers. Berber resistance took longer to suppress. Some Berber customs crept into Muslim teachings.

THE QURAN

Followers of Muhammad had the job of preserving his teachings. They wrote his preachings into a holy book called the Quran.

A caliph named Othman ruled from 644 to 656. He read the first copy of the Quran. He was so moved that he ordered other copies sent to the chief mosques in all Muslim cities. The Quran became the word of God told to Muhammad through an angel. It is the basis for Islam.

Teachings of the Prophet Muhammad were written in the *Hadith,* meaning "traditions." The Hadith contains 7,000 principles selected from over 600,000 that tell of Muhammad's daily behavior. These writings are considered a guide to virtuous behavior.

True believers try to follow the conventions, or Sunna, set by Muhammad in the Quran and Hadith. Muhammad was to be the last of the prophets, or the "Seal of the Prophets." The two writings, particularly the word of God in the Quran, became the core of moral, spiritual, and social life in most Muslim countries, including Libya.

ISLAMIC BELIEFS

Uneducated North African Berber tribes practiced more of a cult than a religion. They believed in *jinns*, or spirits, and "the evil eye." They worshipped saints and had sacrificial ceremonies so the saints would bring them good fortune.

Muslims believe in one God. Rather than gods for various missions, Muhammad used the Arabic term Allah to signify a supreme being over all time and all people. The idea was to honor the message of God instead of the messenger.

The Muslim God is fair and forgiving. That is why Muhammad was sent with messages telling how people could reach Paradise after death. Life on earth is only a testing ground for life to come. People are to do their best and be of service to others to gain entrance into Paradise. Above all, they are to put their faith in God's will to be just.

Heavenly angels note each person's good and bad acts. On their last day on earth, or judgment day, people will receive an account of these deeds. People with good records are given their book in the right hand. They go to heaven. Wicked people who receive their book in the left hand, go to hell. Hell means an afterlife of pain and suffering. Heaven to Muslims is a cool, rich garden of savory fruits. There are running brooks and sweet smells—the opposite of life in the desert.

The Quran supplies the Islamic moral and ethical code. It dictates that people are to be honest, patient, hard-working, and generous. Mistreatment and disrespect are condemned. The writings emphasize honor to parents and protection for orphans, widows, and wives from their husbands. Gambling, money-lending, and sex outside marriage are prohibited, as is consuming pork and alcohol.

As in the Bible, the Quran outlaws cheating, adultery, killing, and thievery. Punishment for these crimes gives back to the criminal what that person has done to another. "An eye for an eye" follows the Old Testament law of revenge with justice. Stealing is met with cutting off a hand. A thief stealing for his hungry family gets a lighter sentence, such as repaying the money.

WORSHIP

Muslims pray in houses of worship called mosques. Mosques are little more than public halls where prayers are conducted. Their meaning as holy places is limited. The word mosque merely identifies it as "a place of worship."

Still, Muslims have built grand mosques. Strict religious codes ban any decorations illustrating living beings, such as people or animals. Instead, there are usually colorful designs of flowers and geometric figures. Passages from the Quran often adorn the walls, also.

A bordering courtyard holds the water fountain for ritual

Since it is forbidden to use representations that depict living beings, geometric and other delicate designs are used for decoration in the interior of this mosque.

washing. Muslims must wash their hands, face, arms to the elbow, and feet before each prayer. If they use the bathroom or touch a dog, they must wash to become pure again.

Mosques are quite simple on the inside. A recessed wall, or *mihrab*, points to Mecca. At least one minaret, or mosque tower, holds the *muezzin*. Muezzins are people who chant the call for prayer. The only other formal areas of the mosque are a pulpit for the leader of the congregation, and a lectern to hold the Quran.

Mosques are cared for by the local community. Muslim religious leaders are not invested with special authority, like priests or rabbis. Islamic officials earn their place with superior learning of the Quran. An *imam*, or leader, guides the people in prayer. Imams with the most authority are *gadis*. Gadis are judges who interpret religious law. They and other religious teachers hold a special place within the community.

Artists' representations of Islam show a muezzin calling people to prayer (left), as they still do, and Mecca (right).

"FIVE PILLARS OF THE FAITH"

Muslims are required to carry out "five pillars," or duties, to prove their faith in Islam.

Shahadah, or testimony. A basic reasoning of Islam is the belief that "There is no God but God (Allah), and Muhammad is his Prophet." Certain ceremonies require repeating this statement. The imam answers the statement by declaring the speaker a Muslim.

Salat, or prayer. Muezzins call Muslims to prayer five times a day, at dawn, noon, midafternoon, sunset, and dusk. People can pray wherever they are—in the field or mosque. However, they must follow the rituals of prayer. The imam faces Mecca with rows of men behind him. Women, usually not as welcome at the mosque, stand behind the men. Everyone prays by reciting

A camel driver at prayer

portions of the Quran. At certain times, they kneel with their foreheads on the floor.

The Friday midday call is the main prayer of the week. The imam gives a short sermon and announces any important news. Friday has become as important as the Christian Sunday or Jewish Saturday. Shops and government offices close. After prayers, people crowd the main streets and parks on cool days.

Sawm, or fasting. The ninth month of the Muslim calendar is Ramadan, the holiest time of the year. Ramadan celebrates when the first chapters of the Quran were imparted to Muhammad. From dawn to dusk, most Muslims cannot eat, drink, or smoke. Only pregnant women, children, travelers, and those who are in battle or sick are relieved of these restrictions.

Ramadan brings problems for those who do manual labor. The fast comes eleven days earlier each year on the Muslim lunar calendar. When it falls in the summer, some workers faint from lack of food. Others have hot tempers to match the weather. Wealthy people are able to slow their work or close businesses to avoid discomfort.

Libya is one of the most strict Islamic countries. Cafes close

Present-day Mecca in Saudi Arabia

during the day. But at night, they bustle with crowds breaking the fast.

Hajj, or pilgrimage. The Quran charges that all able Muslims make at least one pilgrimage to Mecca for prayer. Often, the journey climaxes a lifetime of working and saving. Many travelers hope to die in Mecca and go to Paradise.

Pilgrims must be in Mecca by the sixth day of the month. Several rituals mark the pilgrimage. Pilgrims begin by bathing outside the city. The men put on white seamless garments. Women wear black robes and veils. Neither can shave or cut their hair or nails.

One of the most important ceremonies of Ramadan includes encircling the Kaaba seven times and touching or kissing the blessed black stone embedded in the wall. The stone is the last trace of pilgrimages made by the Prophet Abraham before Muhammad. Legend says the stone was originally white. But it turned black from the "sins of man."

There are many days of prayer and trials. One test challenges pilgrims to run from hill to hill. Unfortunately, the hot sun helps many of the older runners reach Paradise sooner.

The final or tenth day of Hajj is for celebration throughout the

Islamic world. At the Feast of Sacrifice, worshippers slaughter a goat, camel, or sheep and offer its meat to the poor. Prosperous families slaughter two sheep. One is for the poor. The other is cut, dried, and canned for use during the rest of the year.

Worshippers who complete the pilgrimage are honored by adding "al Hajj" before their name. In the late 1970s, about twenty-five thousand Libyans took part in the hajj each year. Their numbers reflect a greater percentage than from other North African nations.

Zakat, or almsgiving. Charity can be required or voluntary. Libyan Muslims originally taxed personal property and used the money for the poor. Then, discovery of oil and the revolutionary government led to public welfare programs. Now, almsgiving has lost some of its importance. Free-will charity still exists. However, laws state that givers cannot deprive their families of their inheritance by donating money.

ISLAMIC SECTS

Islam has become divided into sects through generations. The two largest divisions are the Sunni and the Shiites.

The largest branch of Islam is the Sunni. These are the most traditional Muslims. They hold the Quran and the traditions of Muhammad as sacred. Sunnis were tribespeople who elected caliphs to succeed Muhammad.

Shiites believe Islamic leadership is hereditary. They revere Muhammad's son-in-law, Ali, as his successor. Shiites accept only the Quran and some of the Hadith as sacred.

Islam strongly bans any worship of saints. Modern Libya takes this ban seriously.

The nineteenth-century Sanusi movement drew considerable support among desert tribes of Cyrenaica. The Sanusi movement was successful in rallying the tribes around *sheikhs*, or religious teachers, in the nineteenth century. Sheikhs were appointed by the Grand Sanusi, Muhammad Bin Ali al Sanusi. Religion gave Libyan tribes a unity of purpose. Together they formed the primary resistance to European colonization. Nevertheless, their strength waned after Italian occupation and essentially ended with the revolution.

Sanusis followed a devout and puritanical form of Islam, called Sufi. Believers were expected to live pious lives, help others, and work.

Traditional tribes of Cyrenaica and Fezzan had the greatest exposure to Sanusi Islam. Religion became the basis of their culture. In the past, anyone who worshipped Allah in a different way from the Sanusi was killed. Fortunately, Islam is less harsh today.

QADDAFI'S ISLAM

Qaddafi sees religion as a way to bring people together for a stronger nation. Religion and government are one, and Islam is the proper religion for all Arabs or anyone who thinks correctly. Qaddafi made the Sunni version of Islam the offical state religion.

A major goal of Qaddafi's government has been to reinstate pure Islamic values into everyday life. The Quran is its guiding force. Legal codes governing daily conduct have been adapted from the *sharia*, or religious law. In 1977, the General People's Congress announced that all future laws were to be based on the Quran.

وصول النبي صلى الله عليه وسلم الى اليم الابيض النبي في نواحيه ملائكة كثيرة

حضرت رسالتبناه عليه السلام آق دكن داروب اطرافدن جوق ملائكة واسرايف اول محلدر

The government closed bars and nightclubs after the revolution. Smoking was discouraged. Entertainment thought to be too arousing or morally offensive was banned. A series of enacted punishments reflected Quranic thinking. One law permitted flogging for anyone breaking the fast of Ramadan. Another directed that armed robbers were to lose a hand and foot. The law even limited Libyan men from marrying non-Libyan women.

All people in Libya adhere to prohibitions on gambling and alcohol. Strict bans extend to households of foreign diplomats.

Some Qaddafi policies have caused confusion. Libya began using the Islamic calendar in 1969. The calendar began July 16, 622, when the Prophet Muhammad first made his flight from Mecca to Medina. Therefore, it is not tied to seasons, as is the Western Gregorian solar calendar. The Islamic calendar has 354 days and 12 months that are between 29 and 30 days in length. That is 11 days shorter than the Western calendar, 12 in leap year.

Qaddafi decided to revise the calendar after the Cultural Revolution. He changed the starting date to June 8, 632, when Muhammad died. The new Islamic calendar is followed by the media and for religious practices. Everyday business, especially with foreigners, is conducted by the Gregorian calendar.

Many Libyan religious leaders oppose Qaddafi's strict code over the Quran and Hadith as interpreted in the *Green Book*. But his government has made an impact. In a 1977 poll, Libyans said they preferred religious radio programs over all others.

Libya's economy is based on its oil,
first discovered in the Libyan Desert
in 1959. Left: Burning off
natural gas is called "flaring."
Below: Installing a new well

Chapter 7

THE LAND AS PROVIDER

OIL BOOM

Seventh-century Japanese called it "burning water." Early Persians feared the unusual flames it leaked from the Zagros Mountains. But twentieth-century Libyans knew they had "black gold."

In 1959, the first major oil supply was discovered in the Libyan Desert. The timing was perfect for Libya. The automobile was in its prime, and automobiles needed oil. More countries wanted to change from pollution-causing coal to oil as their main energy source. Oil was to become the key to Libya's economic future. Small Libya, with a population about the size of metropolitan Chicago, was to make its mark on the world with an abundant oil supply.

Discovery of oil influenced Libya's economy more than any event in its recent history. Before oil, Libya relied on aid from Great Britain and the United States to bolster its weak economy. There were few known mineral resources. The future looked grim.

With oil profits, Libya had regular funds to plan for its future. Money from Libyan oil changed every fiber of society.

New wealth is moved in a traditional way,
as a horse and cart are used to pull a tank of fuel.

Individual salaries soared from $40 a year in 1951 to $6,310 per year by 1976. Libya went from being one of the poorest countries to having one of the highest standards of living in the world.

The country spent money from oil profits on government programs to help the people and strengthen the military. According to law, Libya budgeted 15 percent of oil income as reserves each year. Seventy percent was set aside for development projects.

Oil money built roads and airports and improved seaports. Better communication connected Libya's scattered population. The country developed greater linkage with the outside world.

The government also provided social services and utilities where there were none. City and rural towns improved with the opening of clinics, schools, and upgraded housing. Many people were employed to coordinate these programs.

Before the discovery of oil, there were few city jobs. Most people farmed. When farmers came to the city for work, they were forced to live in rundown houses called *barrakas*. Barrakas were mud huts covered with bits of sheet metal, wood, and tar paper from junk piles. People who lived in these huts had no privacy. But they had no money to move elsewhere.

With the discovery of oil, most barrakas disappeared. The government built thousands of new homes and low-rise buildings. Some even had television antennas.

Money for luxuries became available with more people having jobs in the city. Now there was demand for factories to manufacture appliances and other household goods. New shops sparkling with glass, steel, and concrete opened to sell these goods. They also sold modern products from foreign countries. Radios were favorite items. People could hear religious and government programs without having to know how to read.

Oil profits touched rural life as well. The government dug new wells to increase the limited desert water supply. Farmers now had machinery and chemical fertilizer to grow better crops.

Four hundred million trees were planted. Each desert tree was sprayed with oil before it went into the ground. "Black gold" helps firm the shifting sands, allowing the tree to grow.

DEVELOPMENT OF THE OIL INDUSTRY

Within two years of the first major oil strike, oil was ready for export. More oil was discovered in the Surt Basin, a major oil field southeast of the Gulf of Sidra, and Sarir, southeast of the Surt Basin fields. Several minor deposits developed in northwestern Tripolitania. In all, there are some thirty major oil fields and twenty less productive fields in Libya.

Libyan oil was in great demand. The crude oil had less sulphur

The congested port of Tripoli cannot keep up with shipments and boats sometimes have to wait days just to offload.

than oil from neighboring countries. This oil produced less pollution and less wear on engines.

Additionally, Libyan oil was closer to European markets than other eastern Mediterranean oil ports. Oil went directly from oil fields to foreign ships. And ships could go directly home instead of around Africa or through the Suez Canal.

Pipelines were quickly built to transport oil from oil fields to Libyan ports. Tripoli and Banghāzī seaports handled oil, as well as most of the cargo in and out of Libya. The ports at Es'Sider, Ra's Al Unūf, and Marsā al-Buraygah dealt with oil only. As of 1978, pipelines zigzagged from different oil fields to these five export terminals. Libya became the sixth leading oil-producing country in the world.

At first, foreign companies, from such countries as the Netherlands, Great Britain, France, Italy, and the United States,

*Left: An oil derrick   Right: A seismographic
crew measures vibrations within the earth*

owned much of Libya's oil. After the revolution, there was a
movement to have the oil industry run by Libyans. Foreign oil
companies were given the choice of allowing Libyan participation
in governing their business or becoming nationalized.

Today, the government either owns or jointly operates all oil
companies. Decisions about oil policy are guided by the state oil
company, Libyan Petroleum Company (Lipetco). Decisions about
production and pricing policies for all Middle Eastern, Latin
American, African, and Asian oil producers are made collectively
by the Organization of Petroleum Exporting Countries (OPEC).

Initially, Libya needed outsiders. Foreign companies had the
technology and workers to develop and manage the oil industry.
Libyans were mostly untrained and unskilled. Even though Libya
expelled many foreigners in the late 1970s, the country still relies
on outside engineering and technical skills. The over ten thousand
Libyan oil workers are mainly manual laborers and drilling crews.

The presence of foreign workers introduced new customs into Libya. Libyans worked long days with little monetary reward. No one thought to take vacations, buy luxury items, or have leisure time. And Arabs were accustomed to the heat.

But Americans and Europeans complained about conditions even though their pay was high. They were expected to work eight- to ten-hour days in around-the-clock shifts.

To make foreign workers happier, they were flown to resorts along the Mediterranean after many weeks on the job. Lively clubs opened to entertain the visitors. Better food was flown in from Tripoli. To prevent dehydration from the sun, workers drank several gallons of distilled water a day. Workers and their families received air conditioners in their trailer houses. There were also swimming pools and movies.

Many foreign workers have gone, and so have the clubs and movies. And since the early 1980s, Libya's oil production has declined. Yet, a major goal of the government is to educate enough Libyans to eventually replace the remaining foreign workers.

The shortage of skilled workers also affects services arising from the oil boom. Many foreigners, particularly from Islamic countries, are imported to staff schools, hospitals, and construction as well as oil production.

Another government objective is to vary Libya's economy. Currently, oil accounts for about 53 percent of the country's economy and 95 percent of all exports. However, in 1979, oil supplies were projected to last only another thirty-three years. By developing industrial and agricultural resources, Libyans want to rely less on oil, and less on the outside world, to survive.

A mill, using imported raw material, produces Egyptian cotton.

INDUSTRY AND THE LAND

The oil industry spawned an interest in factory-made goods. At the same time, rural artisans preferred work that would bring more money. As a result, production of traditional handcrafts declined.

The government set up training centers to help the remaining artisans practice their trade. In these centers, workers receive low-cost raw materials. Then the government buys most of the finished crafts for resale or export. Local government stores in the old markets display colorful rugs, pottery, leather goods, fabrics, and copperware.

Apart from oil, Libya has few natural resources to build industry. Manufacturing employs only 20 percent of the country's labor force. With few factories, most raw materials are sent to other countries to be made into products and imported into Libya.

Left: Hides and wool are processed for export. Right: A cement factory

Before the revolution, manufacturing centered around products for home use. Crops and livestock were processed into carpets, tobacco, beverages, simple metals, and leather goods. Factories made olive oil, macaroni, tomato paste, and packed dates. Luxury factory-made items were imported.

The revolution brought new interest in local production. Greater food production, textiles, fertilizer, and electric cables became government projects. Although the major export by far is oil, Libya does sell livestock, olive oil, hides, and textiles abroad to such countries as West Germany, Spain, Italy, and Japan.

Even though oil is the most important resource, iron ore presents a potential industry. One of the largest deposits in the world was found in the wadi ash in Shati valley near Sabhah in Fezzan. However, Libya needs a railroad from the valley to the coast to mine the ore. Libya eventually could become independent thanks to iron and steel production.

Another area for future development is the construction industry. Libya has scattered deposits of gypsum, limestone, cement rock, salt, and building stone located near major population centers in Tripolitania and Cyrenaica.

One industry the government wants to develop is nuclear power. Many students are sent abroad to learn nuclear engineering. Libya has an agreement with Argentina to search for uranium. Many countries refused to assist Libya with its nuclear plans. They fear nuclear energy would be used for weapons rather than for peaceful purposes.

FARMING THE LAND

Even with profitable oil industry, Libya is mainly a farming country. Before independence, over half the population farmed. Since that time, figures have dropped to 18 percent, still a sizable number. Yet Libya does not produce all the food needed by its people—a goal the government wants to attain very much.

Part of the problem is the continual water shortage. To remedy this problem, the government has acquired unused land to develop farms. They have trained farmers in modern farming skills, planted crops, and begun large irrigation projects to tap underground water supplies.

The largest undertaking for helping Libya feed its people independently is the "Great Man-Made River" (GMR) water pipeline. By 1991 Phase I of the plan was completed, pumping huge underground water supplies in the southeast desert to Mediterranean coastal areas. In 1989 Phase II was announced, which will bring water farther west toward Tripoli.

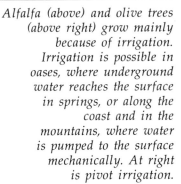

Alfalfa (above) and olive trees (above right) grow mainly because of irrigation. Irrigation is possible in oases, where underground water reaches the surface in springs, or along the coast and in the mountains, where water is pumped to the surface mechanically. At right is pivot irrigation.

Crops are grown along the coast and on oases in the south. The government requires farmers to plant at least 25 percent of their land with cereals. Barley is a traditional crop harvested throughout Libya. Large barley fields can be seen on farms around Tripoli. Gentle wheat fields line the coast. Millet grows in the southern oases.

Almost every Libyan farm has an orchard. Tangerines and lemons dot many of the trees. Some farmers plant almond, date, apple, fig, and olive trees.

Vegetable cultivation is limited to irrigated areas. Farms around Tripoli and Az Zāwiyah grow potatoes, onions, peanuts, and

A livestock market in the city (left) and one in the desert (right)

tomatoes. Most of these crops are grown for local use. Only some, like dates and olives, are exported or traded.

Livestock holds the greatest promise for meeting Libya's needs for meat, poultry, and dairy products. The large amounts of livestock also mean Libya is an important exporter of hides and wool. Farmers are raising larger numbers of sheep, chickens, and cows. Goat and camel herds are common, but decreasing.

Bedouins in the desert breed camels for their meat. They make camel milk into a rich cheese. They sell camel hair to city artisans, who weave the strands into rugs and the white sheets, called *holis*, used in traditional Muslim dress. Selling camel products at the market gives Bedouins a reason to mix with city dwellers.

Contrasting lives of Libyans can differ greatly from rural living (above) to urban life in Tripoli (below).

Chapter 8

CONTRASTING LIVES

Libya had always been a land of divided people. Urban dwellers lived apart from villagers and tribespeople. Each group had its place in the country.

Then independence and the discovery of oil began to blur these distinctions. Better paying jobs lured larger and larger numbers of people to cities, especially after the revolution.

The new government wanted the allegiance of city and village folks. It claimed tribes were a threat to national unity and should be disbanded. The government made laws to curtail tribal loyalty. It provided equal services that offered all groups advancement. They brought city services, such as medical clinics and schools, to oases.

Caravans were replaced by newly paved roads and efficient bus service linking cities and villages. Three international airports and the national carrier, Libyan Arab Airways, brought Libyans to places they had never explored. Airlines connected coastal cities with the Saharan town of Ghāt and other winter getaway spots. Also, modern planes flew to countries in Africa, Asia, and Europe. Libyans were on the move.

Pressures from these events did much to dissolve the city, tribal, and village structures previously known to Libyans. Still, traditional values persist. And new technology and industrial expansion live side by side with ruins of ancient civilizations.

CITY LIFE

Initially, urban Libyans lived in areas called quarters. Many families resided close together for centuries. Leaders from each quarter represented their families in government.

Europeans brought their own style of living. They built separate houses with private gardens along wide streets. Wealthy Libyans copied their housing. The old quarters gradually became areas for the poor.

The new government has removed most of the slums. It responded to overcrowding with blocks of modern apartments. However, traditional homes still maintain old family customs and the sense of privacy Libyans cherish.

CITY HOMES

Traditional homes have walls around them for privacy and to protect the women. The house is divided into separate sections for men and women. Children have their own bedrooms, and can go into either section. As youngsters, they stay more with the women.

Rooms are divided by function. There is usually a living room, dining room, bathroom, bedrooms, and kitchen. Family rooms are not accessible to guests.

There are separate rooms for guests and for family. Guests have

Walls surround homes for privacy, whether the houses are separate (right) or in a group (left).

their own bathroom, bedroom, and receiving area. Invited guests are usually family and friends. While Libyans are friendly to strangers, they rarely invite them to their homes.

Inside the homes are tile gardens, where the children play. Tiles are easily watered to keep the garden cool on hot days. After sand storms, the tiles are swept clean. Some gardens have fountains for decoration. City people have running water in their homes. Water comes from natural wells.

CITY STREETS

Libyan cities are much like western cities. Cars and taxis crowd the streets. Modern office and apartment buildings dot the skyline. What is unusual is the contrast between old and new. With all Libya's advances, donkey-driven water carts can still be seen in downtown Tripoli, side by side with modern automobiles.

Tripoli is a clean, modern city and a major port. Some of its sections can be very congested with traffic.

TRIPOLI

Tripoli is the capital of Libya and its largest city. It is a clean, lively city and major port. Modern Tripoli has quality hotels and air-conditioned buildings. There are factories and canneries. The center bustles with shopping arcades and car dealers. Everywhere, billboards in Arabic encourage the revolution.

Two boulevards lined with palm trees, sidewalk cafes, and shops follow Tripoli's scenic harbor. They wind from new construction to the large castle that once defended the city. The fortresslike structure houses a museum of Roman artifacts.

One of the city's chief forms of entertainment is the Tripoli International Fair. Exhibitors from around the world show examples of their handicrafts, commerce, and industry. There are cultural and technical exchanges. In addition, there is also an amusement fair with toys and rides for children.

*Top: The fortifications
of the Red Castle,
which once defended Tripoli
Left: Banners and
neon signs in Arabic
Above right: At the
ocean near Tripoli,
salt is collected.*

A Roman arch at the entrance to the Old City

The old Roman quarter nearby remains almost intact. Visitors enter through a marble triumphal arch built around A.D 163. Inside the Old City are narrow winding streets, cafes, and, of course, the enormous markets, or *souks*. Clusters of shops and stalls offer gold and jewelry and Arab handicrafts along with radios, appliances, and auto parts. A large covered market has stalls of fresh fruits, vegetables, and meats. Animal carcasses hang uncovered, so a buyer can point to the portion to be cut for the midday meal.

Brightly colored mosques are found throughout all Libyan cities. They function as cultural centers and meeting places, as well as houses of worship. The towering Italian churches, closed since the revolution, serve as gathering points for members of peoples' congresses.

Scenes of Tripoli, clockwise from upper left: a new building under construction; a former Italian cathedral, now converted into the Gamal Nasser Mosque; buildings near the port; and a souk

The interior of a bank (left) and children playing in a new housing area (right) in Banghāzī

BANGHĀZĪ

Banghāzī is Libya's second-largest city, and holds half the people of Tripoli. Libyans call it "The Water City" because of the many ponds that form over the salt marshes surrounding the city.

King Idris made Banghāzī one of Libya's original capital cities. Now Banghāzī is Libya's oil capital. The Jebel Zelten oil fields lie just south of the city. Pipelines extend to oil tankers in this eastern seaport.

Oil money has not reached everyone in this city. Shantytowns of poor people contrast with mosques, apartments, and office buildings dotting the skyline. The Banghāzī campus of the University of Libya has unusual modern architecture and extensive collections. Yet, people are less cosmopolitan here. Many men and women wear traditional white barracans.

A rural village in Darnah

MISRĀTAH

Misratah, once Libya's third-largest city, lies on the west side of the Gulf of Sidra. Misratah gained fame as the stopping-off point for caravan routes. Today, Misratah is known as the center of Libya's carpet industry. Bustling souks display brightly colored rugs from local artisans.

RURAL LIFE

Rural Libyans generally had one of two lifestyles. Nomad tribespeople moved in bands. Their homes were clusters of tents. Farmers lived in stone houses grouped together in villages.

In the 1970s, the government tried to convert the nomads into villagers. Unclaimed land was confiscated. Long-standing villages thought unprofitable were moved. Tribes were scattered. Viable villages were modernized. Former rural village farms and houses received electricity, water, radio, and even television.

Yefren, a Berber town in the mountains of Tripolitania

Sabhah, an ancient oasis settlement, was given electricity, schools, hospitals, and an international airport. The town grew to a city of over 100,000 people with a 3,000-line telephone system. Major irrigation projects made this and other desert communities, like Al Kufrah, bloom.

Some tribes beside the Touareg have defied government attempts to disband them. One unusual Berber tribe lives in caves cut into the hills near Gharyān. These people dug homes about fifty feet (fifteen meters) into the rock. Their homes are warm in winter and cool in summer. The cave homes contain separate rooms for eating, cooking, sleeping, and storage. People sleep on thin straw mats laid on stone slabs.

ANCIENT CITIES

The ancient cities of Sabratah and Leptis Magna attest to the glory of the Libyan land during Roman times. Today, visitors see only ruins—broken walls, cracked columns, and remains of foundations. But the crumbled stones tell of a time when life was prosperous under the Romans.

Greco-Roman ruins of Sabratah

Sabratah lies forty miles (sixty-four kilometers) west of Tripoli. There, archaeologists uncovered houses, temples, baths, and theaters. Statues of marble from Greece and Italy were still in place. Sabratah's theater was considered the largest in North Africa. The semicircular tiers could seat five thousand people. Viewers went to their seats through a maze of tunnels and staircases.

The largest bath in Sabratah still has its heating and drain pipes in place. A large public toilet is part of the bath.

The most telling treasure of Sabratah is its amphitheater. Amphitheaters were the center of activity in Roman days. The arena held official processions and courageous gladiators. Passageways under the arena either led to seating above or contained cages of wild animals for special events. A great sport was to pit criminals against these beasts. Christians were

The amphitheater (left) and a triumphal arch (right) in Sabratah

considered criminals back then. Much Christian blood was shed in this amphitheater during the second and third centuries.

Leptis Magna was a trading city set on a hill sloped toward a large harbor about 75 miles (121 kilometers) east of Tripoli. Living quarters were on the hill and two main city streets were below.

Excavations uncovered an amphitheater, racetrack, public baths, administrative buildings, and columns with statues. All buildings originally were made of limestone. But the Roman Emperor Septimus Severus ordered all the buildings decorated with green, gray, and red marble.

Leptis Magna was fortunate enough to be located near a constant water supply. Roman engineering made the most of the heavy winter rains. Romans constructed the great Wadi Libda to hold water. There are remains of the aqueducts from the wadi that carried water to city baths.

As the Roman Empire waned, the two cities began to die. When Arabs arrived in the seventh century, they concentrated their efforts on Tripoli, a more secure city for trade. Libyan history moved on. However, the legacy of the past lies in these ruins and those yet to be uncovered.

In Leptis Magna, excavations uncovered an
amphitheater (above) and other ruins (below).

Faces of Libya: an Arab horseman;
a Touareg from Ghadamis; migrant workers
from Fezzan; and a student wearing a
headscarf in place of a veil

Chapter 9

THE CHANGING FACES
OF LIBYA

Libya has one of the fastest-growing populations in the world. The government encourages a high birthrate. Improvements in health care, hygiene, and nutrition have changed the face of Libya's population. Libya has a young population. Once the very young and old suffered most from illnesses that plague poor countries. Now Libyan children live into adulthood. Fifty percent of Libyans are under age fifteen. Less than 10 percent are over age fifty.

PEOPLES OF LIBYA

Libyans are mainly a mixture of Arabs and Berbers. These Arabic-speaking people make up about 90 percent of the population scattered throughout Libya. The other 10 percent include Berbers in the west, Touareg and Tebou in the south, black Africans on the southern oases, and other groups that have either been part of Libya's past, such as Greeks, Maltese, Italians, and Jews, or foreigners in Libya's work force.

101

ARABS

Arabs are found mainly clustered around the urban areas of Tripoli and Banghāzī. They either work for the government and industry, or they farm. But they are among the Bedouin tribes in the desert, too.

Some Bedouins move with their herds, searching for grazing land. They roam in the summer, then settle for the winter. Many more live in farm villages. These villages provide a home for younger tribespeople who follow their herds.

BERBERS

True Berbers retain older customs and speak only the Berber language. They are the largest non-Arab minority. Still, they comprise only 4 percent of the Libyan population. This percentage increases when Berbers who speak both Arabic and Berber are added.

Berbers live in small, secluded villages in western Libya. However, there is one settlement in the Cyrenaican town of Awjilah. Here women keep their Berber language and customs from passing into Arabic. The men dress and speak like Arabs as they conduct business in public, but they conceal their women, according to tradition. Thus, the women only speak Berber—and so does each new generation.

Berbers have light complexions. They are a tall people with rugged bodies, and they are fiercely proud and independent.

Most Berbers farm or herd and live in single-family households. They identify with their clan or group within the tribe or village. They are part of the Kharidjite sect of Islam. As their numbers are small in Libya, young Berbers often travel to Tunisia and Algeria to locate Kharidjite wives.

TOUAREG

This unusual minority comprises only about 1 percent of the population. Yet they are well known to Arabs. The Touareg practice a magical form of Sunni Islam.

The Touareg are nomads who wander the southwest desert. They stay close to the oasis towns of Ghāt and Ghadamis. Here they are nearer to larger Touareg tribes in Algeria and the rest of the Sahara.

Touareg live in tight-knit tribes. Their tribal history goes back to the days when they joined other nomadic tribes guiding or looting caravans, kidnapping slaves, and raiding other settlements. In those days, Touareg tribes were composed of six tiers, or classes. There were nobles, priests, serfs, mixed bloods, and blacks, and outdoor slaves. Touareg nobles claimed they were the best race on earth. They did not work, but lived off their serfs and from tributes from caravans. Without the caravan and slave trade, the Touareg became extremely poor.

Through the years, proud Touareg men still wouldn't work. They became poets or warriors. Women came to control tribal economy and property. Inheritances passed from woman to woman. Tribal traditions also derived from women, including mandolin and lute playing.

Usually, it is the women who read or write Arabic and Tifinag. Tifinag is the only written language traced to Berber origins. It has sixty characters and can be written in any direction, such as from right to left, or from bottom to top.

Touareg men

At puberty, the Touareg girl is ready for marriage. Her parents present her in a special ceremony. The Touareg men wear the "veil of submission" after marriage. All Touareg dress in ten feet (three meters) of cloth wrapped around the body and over the face and head. Nobles wear cloth dyed blue or black. After many days, the dye leaves a blue haze on the skin. Nobles with blue dye on their skin have been called "blue men." ·

Traditionally, Touareg believed in washing with sand only. Washing with water at any time besides burial was thought to bring a curse. Women applied rancid butter to their hair.

TEBOU

About 1,500 Tebou remain in the southern desert. Where they came from is unclear. However, their language and customs are similar to the Touareg. And they practice Sanusi Islam.

A man from Fezzan

Like the Touareg, Tebou men, rather than women, wear veils. They breed camels and grow date palms.

BLACK AFRICANS

Children of former slaves from southern African communities live with Arabs and Berbers in coastal towns and in the desert. Most came from slave caravans to the Fezzan before 1929. During World War II, many left for jobs in urban centers. Here they hold low-level positions. Those outside the city are farmers or sharecroppers. Their status comes, in part, from the Libyan bias for light-colored skin. However, color prejudice in North Africa is much milder than in the United States. Leaders and members of the monarchy and the revolution have been dark-skinned Saharan Africans.

ITALIANS AND JEWS

At one time, these two groups prospered in Libya. Jewish settlements in Tripolitania and Cyrenaica go back to before

Muhammad. Jews were accepted in the Muslim world. They were taxed, subject to Libyan laws as well as their own religious courts, and otherwise left alone.

The establishment of a Jewish homeland in Israel after World War II caused resentment among Muslims. Their reaction was violent. Attacks on Jews in Tripoli quickly spread across the country. Two years later, most Jews left for Israel. Violence continued. Property of the few Jews left was taken by the revolutionary government in 1970. That government made clear that it wasn't anti-Jewish but anti-Israel. But the persecution was still the same.

Similarly, the government confiscated all property from Italians who stayed after World War II. The RCC wanted to wipe out all reminders of colonialism. Without their possessions, most Italians left. The withdrawal of large Jewish and Italian communities created a severe shortage of skilled workers in Libya. The government had to recruit workers from other countries until enough Libyans could be trained.

FOREIGN WORKERS

Libya offered many benefit packages to attract foreign workers. By 1980, their numbers reached 40 percent of the work force. Two-thirds of these workers were Egyptian, with a sizable number from Tunisia. Over half the teachers of Libyan children were Egyptian.

Many Greek and Maltese workers already owned businesses before the revolution. Now they were joined by some 375,000 recruits from Pakistan, India, Sudan, Morocco, Syria, South Korea, and Thailand, and 100,000 Europeans from Great Britain, Italy, France, Yugoslavia, Germany, Spain, and Poland.

A poster showing the advantages of good housing

At one time, there were more United States citizens. President Reagan called them home in 1986 to protest Libya's support of international terrorism. Generally, the nationality of foreigners in Libya changes with the current political winds.

LANGUAGE

Arabic is the official Libyan language. The government discourages the use of any other languages. Nevertheless, English functions as a second language. Some urban Libyans also speak Italian, French, and some Berber dialects. A few desert tribespeople speak only Berber.

Libyan Arabic is more formal than the Arabic spoken in other North African countries, but it has many dialects. The language has blended with Italian and Berber through the years. Morocco, Tunisia, and Algeria also have their Arabic dialects. Thus, Arabs from different countries often cannot understand one another.

Even within Libya, dialects interfere with communication. Spoken language in Tripolitania and Fezzan is closer to the dialects from Maghrib countries than to Cyrenaican dialects, which resemble dialects in Egypt and the Middle East. City and rural dialects differ as well.

Three levels of Arabic are recognized. Classical Arabic is the language of the Quran. Religious leaders write this form. Literary Arabic is used by the press, in schools, and in formal situations. Colloquial Arabic appears in various regions.

Arabic is a Semitic language closely related to Hebrew. Both are written from right to left. They have many similar words. For example, the word for peace is *shalom* in Hebrew and *salam* in Arabic. English too, has derived many words from Arabic, such as, cotton, algebra, magazine, almanac, alcohol, and alfalfa.

Libyans believe that speaking a common language is critical for Arab nationalism. Qaddafi played a big role in encouraging the United Nations to adopt Arabic as an official language. He also continues to push for Arabic and Swahili, used throughout East Africa, as official languages of Africa.

ROLE OF THE FAMILY

Libyans place the family at the core of all their relationships. Bonds are strong among family members. The family is honored and respected, especially the elderly. Therefore, each member's dignity depends upon the honor of the family. Any unrevenged wrong dishonors the entire family.

Traditional Libyan households include an extended family. A typical living arrangement may be a husband and wife, any unmarried children, and married sons with their wives and children. Widowed or divorced mothers or sisters may complete the group.

Most Libyan families are fairly large

An average Libyan home has six people under one roof. Bedouins extend this number by clustering their tents around those of other family members.

MEN AND WOMEN—TOGETHER AND APART

Men have always had more status than women in Libyan society. Heredity is passed through men. Men hold most jobs outside the home, in business and in government. Housework and childrearing are women's jobs.

Traditional women learn as young girls that they have different responsibilities from men. They are taught to cater to men. In return, men isolate and protect their women.

Isolation of women began when desert life was dangerous. Men have continued the practice into modern times. They based their thinking on interpretations of the Quran, which said women were the weaker sex. Today, scholars dispute the intent of the Quran.

The revolutionary government wants women to be more equal to men. It set up special polling booths to encourage women to vote. It enacted laws to raise their status, particularly in marriage. For example, Islamic law grants men the right to take up to four wives at one time. A newer law requires that men first get permission from their first wife before marrying another.

The revolutionary government, television, and the oil economy have influenced changes for Libyan women. Yet, change has come slowly. How visible Libyan women are depends upon their age, education, and where they live.

Traditional Bedouin women have had greater freedom from seclusion and wearing a veil. Desert villages were already secluded, so women did not need their veils. They participated in village and farm affairs. However, when visitors came, women disappeared. Modern life came to village girls in the form of secondary education and new job opportunities in the cities.

City women have generally led more secluded lives. The wealthier the woman the fewer responsibilities she has had outside the home. Traditional women have their own quarter of the house where no adult male can go. In the streets, they wear veils to cover their faces. They must walk in pairs and always avoid public gathering places and male contact.

The greatest freedoms have come to younger Libyan women. Those under age thirty-five are more modern and rarely wear veils. They are more apt to attend university and afterwards hold a job, as long as it is performing woman's work, such as social work or teaching young children. But their family and the government still expect them to have children and to care for them at home themselves.

Real equality is still far away for most Libyan women; in 1978, only 5 percent worked outside the home. Women are in the university, in the military, and they can work in some professions. Yet, both men and women have problems accepting a woman's place in this traditionally male-oriented society.

MARRIAGE

Marriage is important in maintaining the family structure in Libya. Boys are not considered men until they marry. Sometimes, boys prove they are adults only after having children.

Girls used to be married in their early teens. Typically, they married much older men. A 1973 law forbade a girl from marrying before she was sixteen. Now girls marry at about nineteen and boys at about twenty-seven.

Marriages are a family affair in Libya. They are arranged through social contacts or by a professional matchmaker. Even when a couple is in love, they keep it a secret to preserve the authority of the family.

Islamic law allows a husband to have four wives at one time. But Muslim wives can only have one husband. Muhammad sanctioned the practice during a time when men were frequently killed in tribal warfare. Harems of many wives were necessary to continue the tribe. But he declared that husbands must give equal treatment to each wife. Today, few can afford the separate but equal households required in the Quran.

A few men still take more than one wife. These men usually have strong reasons. The first wife may be unable to have children, or the man may be very rich and want another wife.

WEDDINGS

Libyan weddings last a week. The cost of the long celebration for both families, plus gold coins and a chest of clothes, are part of the price the groom pays for his bride. Each day has a different celebration. And each night, the bride wears a different traditional outfit in a different color.

The first three days are for women only. Music is played in the bride's home. Guests eat wedding cakes, drink tea, and dance. The fourth day is henna night. Henna is a powder made from a plant that is mixed with water to form natural paint. The bride puts henna in lovely orange and brown designs on her face, hands, and feet. The marks signify tribal associations. Close family and bridesmaids wear henna wedding designs, also. That way guests know who the bride, the bride's sister, and other relations are. Henna lasts for six months.

Guests give gifts on the fifth night. On the sixth night, there is much singing, dancing, and eating. The bride prepares to go to the groom's house. Here the pair is formally joined in matrimony according to Islamic law. However, the bride does not have to come yet. Her father can represent her at the ceremony.

On the seventh night, the bride goes to the groom's home, where she will live with her dowry after marriage. The groom arrives with a male procession. He is taken into the home, where he sees his bride's face for the first time. Both wear white silk costumes.

The bride uncovers her face. Then the groom gives her traditional gold jewelry as a gift. Everyone goes home, and the bride and groom consummate the marriage. Sometimes, in rural areas, both mothers remain in the house until the marriage is consummated. The bride must be a virgin. Otherwise, the marriage contract is broken and her family dishonored.

After marriage, the wife keeps her maiden name. Fathers and grandfathers choose names for children. Children may have the father's name or a combined name from both parents.

A schoolgirl

In Libya, it is important to try to have children right away. Children are the sign of a prosperous family and a healthy marriage.

EDUCATION

Investment in education first began under the monarchy. But the greatest strides have been made since the revolution. Before independence, only about 10 percent of Libya's population could read and write. Almost all these people were men. Higher education usually meant travel abroad.

By the late 1980s, at least 60 percent of Libyans could read, with a large percentage of those being women. Enrollment at the University of Libya's Tripoli and Banghāzī campuses totaled more than twenty-five thousand.

All education is free to Libyans, including university and vocational training. Students are required to complete twelve

The entrance to the university in Tripoli

grades of schooling. They go to school for thirty-five weeks, six days a week, beginning each September.

School consists of six years in primary grades, three years in middle grades, and three years of secondary school. National exams at the end of each grouping decide who passes into the next program. Students who do not pass repeat their last grade.

Before the revolution, schools were taught mainly in Italian and English. Now Arabic is the language of instruction. Libyan children learn English as a second language beginning in the fifth grade. They learn French in high school.

Religion is an important subject at all levels. Anyone failing the religion portion of national exams fails the entire test. Besides religion, several hours a week are devoted to the study of Qaddafi's *Green Books*.

The government has a goal of 100 percent literacy. To achieve that goal, it built schools in the countryside. Where numbers were small, it constructed mobile classrooms and held classses in tents.

These primary students, through education, will be able to help Libya in the future.

City boarding rooms housed children from remote areas coming to urban schools.

The greatest successes have been in urban areas. In large cities, people tend to go to college. In rural areas, students drop out after high school. Parents in the country are said to send daughters to school only to get enough education to attract a husband.

THE PROMISE OF EDUCATION

Still, education holds the greatest promise for the future of Libya. Schools give Libyans skills to fill jobs held by foreigners. They offer technical training to expand the country's oil-based economy. Education allows Libya to compete with the Western world. The government sees literacy as a way to fulfill Libya's dream to be a classless society and remain independent.

MAP KEY

Adrī	D2	Ma'fan	D2
Ajdābiyah (Agedábia)	C4	Ma'ṭan Bishārah	E4
Al Abyad	D2	Marādah	D3
Al 'Azīzīyah	C2	Marāwah	C4
Al Barkāt	E2	Marsā Sūsah	C4
Al Bu'ayrāt	C3	Marzūq	D2
Al Fuqahā'	D3	Ma'tan Bishārah	E4
Al Ḥammādah al Ḥamrā	C2	Misrātah	C3
Al 'Irq	D4	Mizdah	C2
Al Jabal al Akhḍar, mountains	C4	Musaid	C4
Al Jaghbūb	D4	Nālūt	C2
Al Jawf	E4	Qamīnis	C4
Al Jawsh	C2	Qārat as Sa'bah, mountain	D3
Al Khums	C2	Qaṣr Banī Walīd	C2
Al Kufrah (Cufra), oasis	E4	Qaṣr al Burayqah	C3
Al Marj	C4	Ra's 'Āmir	C4
Al Qaryah ash Sharqīyah	C2	Ra's Azzāz	C5
Al Qaṣabāt	C2	Ra's al Unūf	C3
Al Qaṭrūn	E2	Ra's at Tīn	C4
Al 'Uqaylah (Aghéila)	C3	Rebiana, oasis	E4
An Nawfalīyah	C3	Rebiana Sand Sea	E3, E4
Antalāt	C4	Sabhah	D2
As Sulṭān	C3	Samnū	D2
Aṭ Ṭallāb	E4	Sardalas	D2
At Timīmī	C4	Sarīr Calanscio	D4
Awbārī	D2	Sarīr Tibasti	E3
Awjilah	D4	Sawknah	D3
Az Zāwiyah	C2	Sciuēref	D2
Bardīyah	C4	Shahhāt	C4
Baydā'	C4	Shumaykh	C2
Bengasi (Banghāzī)	C4	Sīnāwan	C2
Bette, mountain peak	E3	Sulūq	C4
Bir al Harash, well	D4	Surt	C3
Brach	D2	Taghrīfat	D3
Bū Nujaym	C3	Tajarḥī	E2
Burayk	D2	Tajūrā'	C2
Buzaymah	E4	Tarbū	D3
Dabdab	D2	Tarhūnah	C2
Dahra	D3	Tasāwah	D2
Daraj	C2	Tāwurghā'	C3
Darnah (Derna)	C4	Tazerbo	D4
Es' Sider	C3	Tījī	C2
Gharyān	C2	Tinghert, plateau	D2
Ghāt	E2	Tmassah	D3
Gulf of Sidra (Khalīj Surt)	C3	Tripoli (Ṭarābulus)	C2
Ḥammādat, mountain	D2	Ṭubruq (Tobruk)	C4
Hūn	D3	Tūkrah	C4
Idehan, desert	D2	Waddān	D3
Idehan Marzūq, dunes	E2	Wādī Bay al Kabīr	C2, C3
Jabal Waddān, mountain	D3	Wādī Zamzam	C2
Jabal an Nārī, mountain	E4	Waha	D3
Jabal as Sawdā', mountain	D3	Waḥat Jālū	D4
Jādū	C2	Wāw al Kabīr	D3
Jardinah	C4	Wāw an Nāmūs	E3
Kemme	E3	Zawīlah	D3
Libyan Desert	D4, E5	Zāwiyat Masūs	C4
Libyan Plateau	C4, C5	Zāwiyat al Baydā'	C4
Madrūsah	E2	Zillah	D3
		Zuwārah	C2

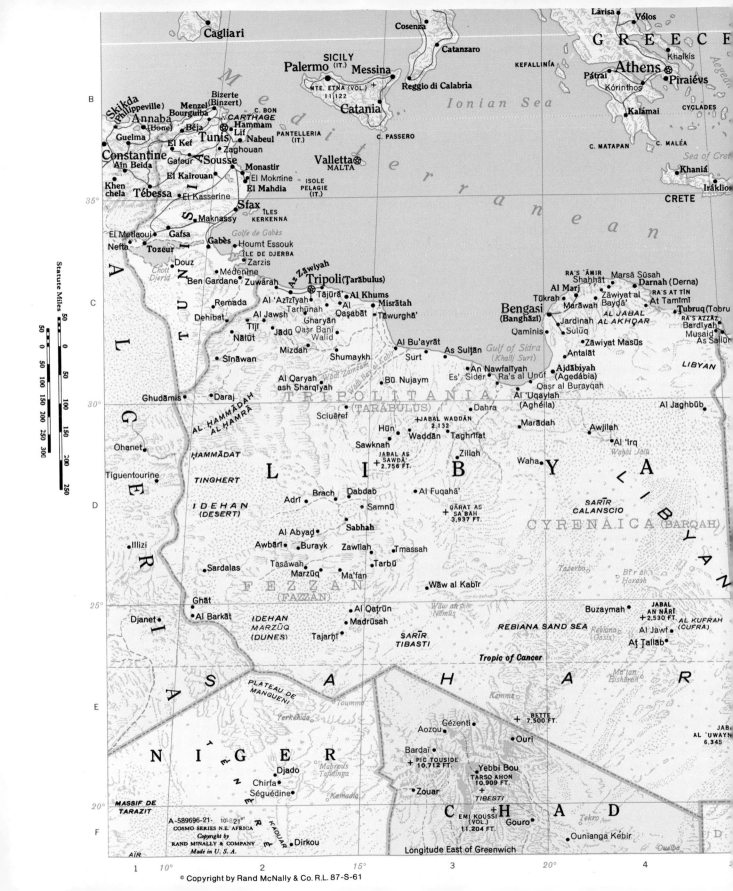

MINI-FACTS AT A GLANCE

GENERAL INFORMATION

Official Name: People's Socialist Libyan Arab Jamahiriya

Capital: Tripoli

Official Language: Arabic is the national language of Libya and many different Arabic dialects are spoken. English was introduced by the British military administration (1943-51), and its use increased with the presence of American and British oil companies. Since Muammar al-Qaddafi came into power in 1969, however, the use of other languages is discouraged by the government.

Government: In September 1969, a republic was formed in a military revolt by the Revolutionary Command Council (RCC) headed by Muammar al-Qaddafi. Prior to the coup, Libya had been a constitutional monarchy. Qaddafi was head of the twelve-member RCC, prime minister, minister of defense, and commander-in-chief. Although there was no legislature nor any elections (the RCC appointed the sixteen-member cabinet) in 1973, Qaddafi created the Arab Socialist Union as Libya's only legal political party. In 1977 Qaddafi redesigned the political system, replacing the republic with what he called a ''jamahiriya.'' This word, which Qaddafi himself coined, is meant to suggest that the people rule themselves without a formal government. Qaddafi resigned from most of his government posts, although he remains head of state and commander-in-chief, and created a system of people's committees and congresses in which people express their preferences for government policy. Today there are thirteen administrative districts, or *muhafazat* which are broken down into small administrative units called *mahallat*. The peoples congresses appoint committees to execute policy at the national level. The governor, *muhafiz*, administers local services.

Flag: Adopted in 1977, the Libyan flag is entirely green, the traditional color of Islam.

National Anthem: ''Allahu Akbar'' (''God is Great'')

Religion: Libya is one of the strictest Islamic countries. Islam is based on the teachings of the prophet Muhammad who, about A.D. 570, urged his followers to believe in one God, Allah, rather than in idols, and to accept him as God's messenger. Muslims follow the writings of the Quran, which dictates the Islamic moral and ethical code. The most traditional Muslim branch is the Sunni, who uphold the Quran and traditions of Muhammad as sacred. Shiites, on the other hand, accept only the Quran as sacred and believe that Islamic leadership passed from Muhammad to his son-in-law, Ali. Muslims pray in mosques, their traditional houses of worship, but daily prayer can take place anywhere. Prayer, or *salat*, is called for five times a day, at dawn, noon, midafternoon, sunset, and dusk. In Libya religion and government are tied closely together. Daily routines, laws, and a general world view all reflect the teachings of Islam.

Money: The dinar is Libya's basic monetary unit. It is divided into 1,000 dirhams. In March 1993, the official exchange rate was 0.176 dinar to $1.00 in United States currency. The Bank of Libya supervises the country's banking system. There are also two specialized state investment banks and four foreign commercial banks.

Weights and Measures: Libya uses the metric system.

Calendar: Libya maintains three calendar systems. In addition to the Western calendar, there is the Muslim calendar, which consists of twelve lunar months and is eleven to twelve days shorter than the astronomical year. The Muslim calendar begins in year 622 of the Western calendar, the year Muhammad fled from Mecca to Medina. The third calendar, instituted in the late 1970s, begins with the prophet Muhammad's death rather than his move to Medina. This calendar, which is in use nowhere else in the world, was devised by Qaddafi to illustrate what he views as the rights of individuals in Islam to interpret religious dictates and customs rather than to follow unquestioning the traditional interpretations. It is not a particularly popular innovation.

Population: 3,637,488 (1984 census); 1993 estimate: 4,500,000; 65 percent urban, 35 percent rural. Close to three-quarters of the population live in the northwest along the Mediterranean, while the remainder congregate on the northeast coast. Arabs make up 90 percent of the population. Berbers, living in small villages, are the largest non-Arab minority.

Cities:

	1980 Census	1988 Estimate
Tripoli.	380,000	591,100
Banghāzī.	279,000	446,250
Misratāh.	102,400	121,700

GEOGRAPHY

Highest Point: Bette Peak, 7,500 ft. (2,286 m) The general elevation of the country is about 2,000 ft. (610 m) above sea level.

Lowest Point: 80 ft. (24m) below sea level

Rivers: There are no permanent or ever-flowing rivers in Libya. Wadis (dry riverbeds) are filled by flash floods during rains, but they dry up quickly due to the arid desert climate.

Oases: The desert is scattered with oases— shady, palm-covered areas fed by underground wells and springs.

Salt Lakes: Called *sabkhahs*, these salt lakes dot the coastline. The primary salt lakes are those of Tawurgha, Zuqarah, and the Banghāzī.

Mountains: There are no true mountain ranges in Libya, but ranges of highlands or *jebels* and plateaus do exist. The limestone plateau, Jabal Nafusah, stretches about 22 mi. (35 km) from east to west and rises to 333 ft. (101 m). Another limestone plateau, al-Jabal al-Akhdar, stretches for about 100 mi. (161 km) on the coast and about 20 mi. (32 km) inland, and reaches about 2,900 ft. (884 m) in height.

Climate: The Sahara Desert and the Libyan Desert of Fezzan cover most of Libya, resulting in extremely hot days and little rain. It has been known not to rain for 200 days straight. Summer temperatures can reach 115 degrees Fahrenheit (46 degrees Celsius) and winter temperatures range from 45 to 86 degrees Fahrenheit (7 to 30 degrees Celsius). Along the coast, climate is moderated by the Mediterranean Sea. Summers are warm and winters are milder than in the inland desert. Average rainfall ranges between 10 and 14 in. (22 to 29 mm) annually. Weather on the coast can be humid, accompanied by hot, dusty, dry, strong winds that commonly last one to four days and causes sudden rises in temperature.

Greatest Distances: North to south—930 mi. (1,497 km)
East to west—1,050 mi. (1,690 km)
Coastline—1,047 mi. (1,685 km)

Area: 679,362 sq. mi. (1,759,540 km²). In terms of land area, Libya is the fourth largest country in Africa and the fifteenth largest in the world.

NATURE

Trees: The cactus is Libya's national plant. Cacti grow throughout Libya, as do date and palm trees. In the semidesert and desert areas, vegetation is sparse. Only 1 percent of Libya is forested. The northern area, al-Jabal al-Akhdar, is the most influenced by the Mediterranean Sea and has a low, fairly dense forest (*macchia*) with juniper, cypress, wild olive, and pine trees primarily.

Animals: The *waddan*, a male gazelle, is Libya's national animal. Other indigenous wild animals include desert rodents, hyenas, foxes, jackals, skunks, and wildcats. Wild ringdove, partridge, lark, prairie hen, finch, eagles, hawks, and vultures are common, as are ducks, gulls, plover, and terns in coastal areas. Poisonous reptiles, such as adder and krait, inhabit oases and waterholes. Insects are common, and migrating butterflies and locusts cross the interior. There is little local demand for fish, but surrounding waters do contain tuna, sardines, and red millet, as well as turtles, lobsters, and crawfish. Sponge beds are also widely available.

EVERYDAY LIFE

Holidays and Festivals:
June 30, Troop Withdrawal Day
September 1, Revolution Day
December 24, Independence Day
Prophet Muhammad's Birthday
'Id al-Sagiir—a feast celebrated at the end of Ramadan, an annual month-long Muslim fast
Dhm al Hijja—celebrates the return of a family member from a pilgrimage to Mecca
'Id al-Ada—a feast of sacrifice commemorating Abraham's offer to sacrifice his son Isaac to Allah

Food: Libyans tend to enjoy their food either highly seasoned or very sweet. The main meal of the day is usually eaten around 2:00P.M. before the daily afternoon rest. Lamb is the meat most often eaten by Libyans and it is usually consumed at the midday meal. Dinner consists of a lighter meal of yogurt and cheese. Pork is forbidden, according to Islam, the national religion. There are two national dishes: *cous-cous*, which is wheat flour kneaded into tiny balls and steamed, then served either plain or sweetend with honey and milk or as a meal with vegetables and lamb; and *tajine*, which consists of wheat, vegetables, and meat mixed into a dough and cooked. Tea is Libya's national beverage. It is generally brewed very strong and served with roasted hazelnuts and sugar.

Housing: Traditional city houses are divided into separate sections for men and women, as well as for guests and family. Two walls surround homes, one for privacy, one to protect the women. Modern high rises now fill the skylines of the cities and even in small villages, TV antennaes can be seen on the homes.

Social Structure: Libyan society is patriarchal in nature. Men have more status than women, and are generally the ones to work outside the home. City women are very secluded and must cover their faces in public. Village women, on the other hand, have greater freedom due to the natural seclusion of their villages. The family is considered the core of all Libyan relationships, and is the foundation of Libya's government and of Islam. The traditional household includes an extended family. Mothers typically arrange their children's marriages, and Libyan weddings often last a week. Islamic law allows a man to have four wives at one time (as long as he provides for them equally), but a Muslim woman may have only one husband at a time.

Dress: European-style clothing is typically worn in cities, yet traditional Arab clothing is also worn. Traditional dress for both men and women includes several layers of loosely fitting clothing worn under a *barracan*. A barracan fastens at the shoulder and under the chin and wraps the body from head to toe.

Culture: Libyan culture centers on folk art and traditions, which are highly influenced by Islam. Weaving, embroidery, metal engraving, and leatherwork—the traditional arts—rarely depict people or animals because Islam prohibits such representation. Geometric and arabesque designs are predominant and are seen in the stucco and tiles of mosques of Libya. Festivals, horse races, and folk dances are traditions that continue to survive. Musical styles are basically Arabic and largely rely on improvisation. Nonreligious literature has been developing since the 1960s; it is nationalistic in character, but shows Egyptian influences. The arts are supported by the government. Libraries include the Government Library and Archives in Tripoli, the Public Library in Banghāzī, and the university libraries.

Sports and Recreation: In rural areas horse racing and *fantasias* (displays of horsemanship) are popular, as are camel racing, a game similar to polo, and hunting with falcons and hawks. In the cities, popular sports include soccer, basketball, boxing, and track and field. Yet the government frowns on spectator sports.

Communication: Libya maintains government-owned telecommunication systems. There are four radio stations that offer cultural programming and literacy lessons. Television stations broadcast for three hours daily. There is one daily newspaper, six weekly newspapers, and seven magazines, all published in Arabic.

Transportation: As of 1986, Libya had 15,954 mi. (75,675 km) of roads. The main artery is a 1,100-mi. (1,770-km) coastal highway between the Tunisian and Egyptian borders, which branches out to coastal towns. Most towns and villages can be reached by road. In the interior, camels are often used for travel. Currently, Libya has no railroads. Tripoli and Banghāzī are the country's major seaports. There are two international airports.

Education: All public education in Libya is free. Completion of twelve grades is required. Religion is taught at all levels. The educational system is divided into six years in primary grades, three years in middle grades and vocational training, and three years in secondary school and advanced vocational training. National examinations determine who advances from one level to the next. Higher education is offered by the government-run University of Libya and is also available free of charge. The state also runs a statewide literacy program for adults.

Health and Welfare: Health care is available free of charge to all Libyans. Most health care is available in hospitals since there are few outpatient or specialized-care facilities. Most medical personnel are non-Libyan. The National Social Insurance Institute operates social security programs, including old-age pensions and workmen's compensation.

ECONOMY AND INDUSTRY

Principal Products:
Agriculture—barley, wheat, citrus fruits, dates, olives, livestock
Mining—oil, natural gas, gypsum
Manufacturing—carpets, textiles, petroleum

IMPORTANT DATES

1000 B.C.—Garamentes tribe conquers Fezzan desert; Phoenicians establish foreign settlements along Libyan coast

950 B.C.—The Berber, Shishonk I, takes control of Libya, beginning a succession of Berber pharaohs known as the Libyan Dynasty, extending close to two hundred years

700-500 B.C.—Three Phoenician settlements are established in Libya that become known as Tripoli or Three Cities

631 B.C.—Greeks found the city of Cyrene in Cyrenaica, which prospers as a Greek trade and cultural center

100s B.C.—Romans conquer Libya and Roman rule continues for several hundred years. By A.D. 400 Romans bring Christianity to Libya

A.D. 400—German barbarians, called Vandals, conquer the area

535—Byzantines overcome Vandals

622—Muhammad flees Mecca for Medina in the Arabian Peninsula

630—Islam is accepted, with Muhammad as spiritual leader; Mecca and Medina become Islamic sacred cities

632—Muhammad dies

710—Introduction of Islam and Arab conquest; Arabs rule until 1500s

1500—King Ferdinand of Spain captures Tripoli; attempts to reintroduce Christianity during the crusades

1551—Ottoman Empire conquers the Spanish and rules formally until 1911

1710—Ahmed Karamanli conquers Tripoli and establishes Karamanli Dynasty

1801-05 and 1812—Barbary Wars

1835—Ottoman Empire overturns Karamanli Dynasty to rule directly

1842—Sanusi order of Islam founded in Cyrenaica by Muhammad Bin Ali al Sanusi

1911—Italians invade Libya and conquer Ottoman Empire; Libyans continue resistance

1922—Italian troops march into Libya under Mussolini and defeat Libyan resistance within a decade

1939—World War II begins

1943—Last Italian forces leave Libya

1951—Libya becomes first country to gain independence through the United Nations; King Idris becomes chief of state

1959—Oil discovered

1969—King Idris ousted in a military revolt led by Muammar al-Qaddafi and the Revolutionary Command Council; Qaddafi takes power

1973—Qaddafi introduces Cultural Revolution

1977—General People's Congress meets with 1,000 delegates selected by local-level people's committees

1981—United States closes Libyan embassy in Washington, D.C., because of Libya's support of terrorism

1984—Great Britain ends diplomatic relations with Libya

1985 — The United States accuses Libya of increasing terrorist activities throughout the world

1986 — The United States orders all Americans to leave Libya and takes part in armed skirmishes in the air over the Gulf of Sidra

1989 — Libya celebrates the twentieth anniversary of Qaddafi's rule; Libya and Egypt embark on a rapid course of reconciliation, opening the borders between the two countries for the first time since 1977

1992 — The United Nations Security Council imposes sanctions against Libya for refusing to surrender suspected agents in various airline bombings; Libya retaliates with destruction of property at foreign embassies

1993 — Qaddafi announces on television that Libya plans to promote tourism

IMPORTANT PEOPLE

Khair al Din (1466?-1547), also known as Barbarossa, Barbary pirate captain who captured Algiers in 1510, became governor, and expanded Ottoman power in the region

Ahmed Karamanli, Turkish pirate who conquered Tripoli in 1710; his family ruled until 1835

Muhammad al Mahdi (d. 1902), son of the Grand Sanusi; took over leadership of the Sanusi order upon his father's death

Omar Mukhtar (d. 1931), Sanusi scholar of the Quran who taught in Cyrenaica and was active in the underground resistance movement against the Italians

Muhammad of Mecca (570-632), Arabian prophet and founder of the Islam religion

Muammar al-Qaddafi (1942-   ), a devout Muslim who led a revolt that overthrew King Idris in 1969; currently head of state and commander-in-chief

Muhammad Bin Ali al Sanusi (1787-1859), Islamic scholar and teacher who established the Sanusi Islamic sect in 1843; called the Grand Sanusi

Muhammad Idris al Sanusi (1890-1981), known as Idris; cousin of Ahmed al Sharif; assumed political and military control of the Sanusi in 1916; proclaimed king of independent Libya in 1951; deposed by Qaddafi in 1969

Ahmed al Sharif al-Sanusi (1873-1933), grandson of the Grand Sanusi; succeeded the Mahdi as leader of the Sanusi order in 1902 and went on to lead a resistance against the Italian occupation in Cyrenaica from 1911 to 1916; turned leadership of Sanusi order over to cousin Idris in 1916 after military defeat by British in Egypt

INDEX

Page numbers that appear in boldface type indicate illustrations

About the Author

Marlene Targ Brill is a free-lance Chicago-area writer, specializing in fiction and nonfiction books, articles, media, and other educational materials for children and adults. Among her credits are *John Adams* and *I Can Be a Lawyer* for Childrens Press; *Washington, D.C. Travel Guide*, a regular column for the secondary publication, *Career World*; and contributions to World Book Encyclopedia's *The President's World* and *Encyclopaedia Britannica*.

Ms. Brill holds a B.A. in special education from the University of Illinois and an M.A. in early childhood education from Roosevelt University. She currently writes for business, health care, and young people's publications and is active in Chicago Women in Publishing and Independent Writers of Chicago.

Ms. Brill would like to thank Layla Kassem for assistance in preparing this book. She also wishes to acknowledge the encouragement of her husband, Richard, and daughter, Alison—two people who particularly crave knowledge and appreciate a good book.